W9-DFR-356

WITHDRAWN

100 PREDICTIONS FOR THE BABY BOOM

The Next 50 Years

100 PREDICTIONS FOR THE BABY BOOM

The Next 50 Years

CHERYL RUSSELL

PLENUM PRESS • NEW YORK AND LONDON

Library of Congress Cataloging in Publication Data

Russell, Cheryl, 1953–
  100 predictions for the baby boom.

  Bibliography: p.
  Includes index.
  1. Economic forecasting—United States. 2. United States—Economic conditions—1981–   3. Social prediction—United States. I. Title. II. Title: One hundred
predictions for the baby boom.
HC106.8.R87 1987   338.5′443′0973   87-2443
ISBN 0-306-42527-0

© 1987 Cheryl Russell

Plenum Press is a Division of
Plenum Publishing Corporation
233 Spring Street, New York, N.Y. 10013

All rights reserved

No part of this book may be reproduced, stored in a retrieval system, or transmitted
in any form or by any means, electronic, mechanical, photocopying, microfilming,
recording, or otherwise, without written permission from the Publisher

Printed in the United States of America

For Rick
who is a baby boomer
and
For Pike
who was not

PREFACE

Without the baby boom, the United States would be a different place. The Vietnam War would have lasted longer. Rock and roll would be less pervasive. The civil rights movement would have changed laws and attitudes more slowly. But women might be further ahead in job status and pay if there had been no baby boom. Housing would be cheaper. The economy would have done better in the 1970s, and people now in their 20s, 30s, and 40s would be making more money.

For the past 30 years, the baby boom generation—all those born between 1946 and 1964—shook American economics, politics, and culture. But the full impact of the baby boom is yet to come because the generation is just now gaining the economic and political power to determine events.

Though the baby boom is a diverse generation linked only by its date of birth, that link is critical. The generation spans 19 years, which means many boomers experience the same things at the same time—going to college, getting a job, marrying, divorcing, buying a house, starting a family. Because of this, the baby boom influences what America's businesses produce, what the media write about, and what the politicans support. It focuses the nation's attention on itself; its concerns become the nation's concerns. Whatever age the baby boom is becomes the nation's age.

This book is about what will happen to the baby boom as it gets older. While there will be many individual variations on the ideas presented here, the book describes the dominant themes of American life that will emerge over the next 50 years because of the aging of the baby boom.

Some of the facts on which this book is based may go against the grain because they are contrary to the way some people live. All of us are uniquely entrenched in our own points of view and guilty at one time or another of assuming that everyone else shares our perspectives. This kind of bias is called an Aunt Jane-ism: "I know that baby-boom women are quitting their jobs to raise families because my Aunt Jane just quit her job." Aunt Jane-isms litter much of today's newspaper and magazine reporting, influencing public opinion and creating a distorted picture of how Americans live. The statistics in this book are not Aunt Jane-isms. They are facts based on nationally representative surveys of the American people. They describe how one generation of Americans lives.

The book begins with predictions about the baby boom's life based on its prevailing lifestyle, and based on the foreseeable events that happen as people age. The rest of the book examines the predictions in more detail. The second chapter, "The Boom," discusses the unusual psychology of the 1950s that created the baby boom. The next section, "Middle Age," describes the baby boom's next three decades—the years devoted to work and family. The final section, "Old Age," describes the baby boom's retirement—the years devoted to leisure and the flight from death.

Many people offered me their ideas and support during the year of labor that went into this project. I would like to thank Tom Parker for his helpful suggestions in shaping the book. Thanks go to Diane Crispell, associate editor of *American Demographics*, for her review of the many numbers. And many thanks to the entire staff of American Demographics, Inc., in particular Peter Francese, Doris Walsh, Penelope Wickham, Caroline Arthur, Nancy Ten Kate, Tom Exter, Brad Edmondson, Joe Schwartz, Mike Rider, Marty Riche, and Bickley Townsend. Without American Demographics—an organization devoted to tracking how Americans live—this book would not exist. Thanks also to my husband Rick Eckstrom, who had to put up with a lot. For that I can't thank him enough.

Cheryl Russell

CONTENTS

Middle Age

Old Age

CHAPTER 1

PREDICTIONS

When the first baby boomer turned 40 on January 1, 1986, it changed the way Americans thought about themselves. How could a "baby boomer" be middle-aged? This country's passionate affair with youth was over.

The middle-aging of the baby boom was inevitable. Equally inevitable are the changes that the middle-aging of the baby boom will force on the American culture. The last time the country's mood changed so dramatically was in the 1950s, when children and teenagers seized power. For 30 years the young ruled American life. Now that era is over. The middle-aged will wield power for the next 20 years.

But middle age does not mean what it used to mean. The baby boom is changing midlife just as it changed teenage life, making middle age more diverse than in the past. Twenty years ago it was a sure bet that a middle-aged American would be married and have teenage children. Today, the middle-aged are single, married, or divorced. Their children might be teenagers or toddlers, and many have no children at all.

The baby boom's middle age will transform the United States in three important ways: It will make the country more conservative, it will make the home the focus of American life, and it will make the nation richer.

The United States stands at the brink of the most affluent decades in its history because of the middle-aging of the baby boom. In a few years, the oldest members of the generation will be at their peak in earning power. Their affluence will benefit American families, communities, and businesses. But it will also tighten the nation's purse strings. Until well after the turn of the century, middle-aged Americans will anxiously protect what they have. Bread and butter issues will be important—taxes, jobs, houses, wages, investments, schools, and welfare and immigration reform will top the nation's economic and political agenda.

"Live for today" was the philosophy of the free-wheeling teenage culture that dominated the United States for the past three decades. Middle-age culture will be more stable, serious, and careful. Teenagers and young adults experiment with life; the middle-aged know more about what they like and don't like. The moderations of middle age are already evident in the nation's growing concern over drinking and driving, drug abuse, pornography, and crime. The huge baby-boom generation now has children to raise, property to tend, and communities to protect.

The home will symbolize the social stability of the next few decades. It will be the center of American life, equipped with VCRs, home computers, compact disk stereo systems, cable television, large-screen and pocket-sized televisions, security systems, answering machines, microwaves, exercise equipment, and a host of new technologies not yet on the drawing boards. Middle-aged consumers, short on leisure time and busy raising children, will spend more time at home. The businesses that catered to the young (such as singles bars, laundromats, and ski resorts) will have to change their strategies. Movie theaters are already giving way to VCRs; restaurants and grocery stores are offering home delivery; the health club is moving into the den; even fashions are changing, as the middle-aged consumer—more concerned with comfort than the latest style—buys clothes that feel good.

The middle-aging of America won't last forever. For the next two decades—from now until 2010—it will glory in its prime. Beginning around 2010, however, there will be another dramatic transformation in the American mood as demographic change dictates yet another way of life. When the baby boom retires, the old will dominate the country. The aging of America will loosen the harsh grip of conservatism, but it will also end the most affluent era in American history. America's old age won't be as rich as its middle age, but it may be more generous. What old age will be like depends on the choices the baby boom is making now.

One thing is certain—a huge generation is getting older. What happens to people as they age is predictable. This makes it possible to predict how the baby boom will fare in middle and old age. Here are some of those predictions.

PREDICTIONS ABOUT THE FAMILY

Nine out of ten baby boomers will marry once.

One in three will marry twice.

A baby-boom marriage will last 23 years, on average.

Half of all baby boomers will divorce once.

One in five will divorce twice.

Only 6 in 100 baby boomers will achieve the ideal family—a lifetime marriage with two children, a boy and a girl.

Only 13% of baby-boom couples will celebrate their 50th wedding anniversary.

Two-thirds of baby-boom households will be married couples by 1995.

Married baby boomers will be the affluent of the decades ahead; single baby boomers will be the poor.

Baby-boom men will be as dependent on marriage as baby-boom women.

Baby-boom husbands will do one-third of the family housework, on average.

Fewer than one-fifth of baby-boom women will spend their lives as housewives.

PREDICTIONS ABOUT CHILDREN

By 1995, most baby-boom women will be sterile.

One baby boomer in six will have no children.

One baby boomer in ten will wish she had children.

One in three baby-boom women will have three or more children.

Record numbers of baby-boom women will have children without a husband.

Most of the baby boom's children will see their parents divorce.

The children of divorced baby boomers will rarely see their fathers.

One-third of the baby boom's children will live with a step-parent.

Baby-boom parents will spend over $100,000 raising their first child.

The baby boom will send its children to private schools unless the public schools improve.

The baby boom will spend $30,000 a year sending a child to college.

Eight out of ten children of the baby boom will go to college.

PREDICTIONS ABOUT WORK

Eighty percent of baby-boom women will be working by 1995.

Most of the baby boom's children will be raised by mothers and fathers who work.

Baby-boom men will work for 33 years, on average.

Baby-boom women will work for 24 years, on average.

In 20 years, one-third of the nation's doctors will be women.

One-third of the nation's business managers will be women in 20 years.

One-third of the nation's lawyers will be women in 20 years.

Working women will earn 74% of what working men earn by 2000.

Baby boomers will work at ten different jobs during their lives.

Fringe benefits will become as important as salary when the baby boom hunts for jobs.

The baby boomers will enjoy working more than they will enjoy watching television.

PREDICTIONS ABOUT MONEY

Most baby boomers will be middle-class.

The older baby boomers will have hundreds of dollars more money to spend each month than the younger baby boomers.

In 1995, only one in ten baby-boom households will make less than $10,000 a year.*

*All earnings figures are adjusted for inflation.

By 1995, one in four baby-boom households will make more than $50,000 a year.

Forty percent of baby-boom households will have money to spend on luxuries.

By the turn of the century, one in ten baby-boom households will make $75,000 or more a year.

College-educated baby-boom men will earn more than $1 million during their lives.

The affluent baby boomers will be those who get out of debt.

Many baby boomers will become speculators in order to increase their wealth.

The baby boom will keep the stock market volatile for the rest of this century.

The earnings of baby-boom men will peak at about $30,000 a year.

Baby-boom women's earnings will peak at about $25,000 a year.

The baby boom will give to charity three times as much money as it does today.

PREDICTIONS ABOUT THE HOME

By the year 2000, three out of four baby boomers will own a home.

Among the homeowners, 90% will own a home like the one in which they grew up.

The baby boomers will spend a lot of time at home.

The baby boom's homes will be electronic castles.

For most baby boomers, real estate will not be a good investment.

The baby boom will make home delivery a big business.

PREDICTIONS ABOUT BUSINESS

The baby boom's vacations will be short, but they will vacation more often than their parents did.

The baby boom will create a new industry that sells them experiences.

The baby boom will do a lot of its shopping by mail.

The buying habits of the baby boom will hurt the nation's shopping malls.

The baby boom will close down many of the nation's movie theaters.

The baby boom will buy imports.

The baby boom will make baseball the sport of the 1990s.

PREDICTIONS ABOUT BELIEFS

The baby boom will become more conservative in middle age.

The baby-boom vote will make a difference for the first time in the presidential election of 1992.

Many baby boomers will polarize into two camps—the fundamentalists and the nonreligious. But most baby boomers will fall somewhere in between.

Most baby boomers will be community volunteers by 1995.

The baby boom will become more liberal in old age.

American social consciousness will rewaken in the year 2010.

PREDICTIONS ABOUT RETIREMENT

Eight out of ten baby boomers will live to age 65.

Most baby boomers will retire before the age of 65.

The baby boom will spend 20 years in retirement.

Nine out of ten retired baby boomers will receive Social Security checks.

Social Security will account for the largest share of the baby boom's retirement income.

The baby boomers will not be able to save enough money on their own for a comfortable retirement.

Two out of three retired baby boomers will receive a company pension.

The baby boomers who continue to live for today will be paupers in old age.

In old age, a minority of baby boomers will move south.

The baby boom will rediscover communal living in the next century.

PREDICTIONS ABOUT AGING

Most baby boomers will feel fat in middle age.

The baby boomers will spend the rest of their lives trying to look young.

The baby boom will create a boom in plastic surgery.

One out of three baby boomers will live to age 85.

The baby boom will search for the meaning of life.

Sixty percent of elderly baby boomers will be women.

Seven out of ten baby-boom women will outlive their husbands.

Baby-boom women will spend 15 years as widows, on average.

On a scale of one to ten, most baby boomers will feel like a "seven" on most of the days of their old age.

The older the baby boomers get, the fewer colds they will catch.

The baby boomers can expect to spend three days a year, on average, sick in bed.

At least one-third of elderly baby boomers will have hearing problems.

One-half of elderly baby boomers will have arthritis.

Heart disease, cancer, and stroke will kill seven out of ten baby boomers.

Medical bills will be the single largest expense of elderly baby boomers.

In old age, 40% of baby boomers will be dependent on friends and relatives to help them with their daily chores.

Many baby boomers will be cared for by their nieces in old age.

The best long-term investment for the baby boom will be to have children.

Baby boomers will buy nursing home insurance.

By the year 2045, one in five baby boomers will be in a nursing home.

One million baby boomers will live to be 100 years old.

The last baby boomer will die in about 2069.

The baby boom will not grow old gracefully. The hysteria has already begun.

CHAPTER 2

THE BOOM

The baby boom was an accident, a coincidence of events. Seventeen million more people were born between 1946 and 1964 than would have been born if the young American women of the postwar years had followed the traditions of their mothers. Without the extra births, those born between 1946 and 1964 would have grown up inconspicuously. Instead, the huge generation—now one-third of all Americans—changed the United States as much as any war, depression, president, or invention. For decades social scientists have been trying to explain why the baby boom happened. They might as well try to explain the hoola hoop—the baby boom was a freak storm of life, a baby fad sparked by the euphoria of victory in World War II.

27

The War took millions of American men thousands of miles away to fight for their lives, and for a way of life. The psychological impact of the War on Americans back home was tremendous. Suddenly the humdrum habits of peacetime life—preparing breakfast, going to the movies, visiting relatives—seemed too good to be true. The men away at war and the women they left behind longed for nothing more than a return to normal family life, thus laying the emotional foundation for the baby boom.

Germany surrendered in May 1945. Japan gave up in August. In the following months, 16 million men came home, igniting a 19-year boom that gave birth to 76 million Americans.

For years, Americans had prayed and prepared for the day when life would return to normal. Nowhere are these longings more evident than in the way businesses exploited them to sell everything from cars to mouthwash. "When you meet again," whispered Nash Motors to its potential customers in 1945.[1] "So sweet to come home to," promised Lysterine Antiseptic to millions of waiting women.[2]

When the men came home the relief was frenzied. "Hold it stars! Listen moon! This is the day, this is the moment, this is forever!" crooned the ads of the flatware company Community Silverplate in 1945.[3]

"Strong brown fingers lift your chin...remember? Two firm lips just right for yours...remember? Your eyes are bright, your heart's flung wide, your world spins round and comes to anchor...for keeps!" For

keeps: Community Silverplate was just one of many businesses poised for what was to come. Its ads played on
the feelings of American women perfectly. Now that the
War was over, nothing was going to come between
Americans and the joys of family life. ''Dare to
dream...dare to cut yourself a slice of heaven. Some day
you'll have it...that storybook house, the crackling
fire.... ''[4]

Husband, house, and baby were the three most important ingredients of the postwar American dream. Not
much more than nine months after the soldiers returned
home, the baby boom began. The first evidence of a
boom appeared in June 1946 as births rose.[5] By the end
of the year, American women were having 338,000 babies each month, 100,000 more per month than in 1945.
The year 1946 ended with a record number of births for
the United States—3.4 million.

That was just the beginning, because few Americans
could resist two firm lips and a slice of heaven. The marriage boom of the late 1940s fueled the fire of the baby
boom, which was to last for nearly two decades, reshap-
ing American traditions. The average age for marrying
dropped for both men and women. Suddenly, the unmarried were an out-of-place minority. In 1946, 2.3 million marriages took place, 29% more than in any prior
year in American history.[6] Another 2 million followed in
1947, and 1.8 million in 1948. Public opinion turned
against the unmarried. By the mid-1950s, more than half
of the American public believed that people who did not
want to marry were sick, immoral, selfish, or neurotic,
according to a survey at the time.[7]

The years of nearly universal marriage following World War II are unique in American history. In 1900, most young women were unmarried. By 1950, only 32% of women aged 20 to 24 were unmarried.[8] During the baby-boom years, most women married before the age of 20.

The thorns among the roses soon drew blood, however. Along with a record number of marriages in 1946 followed a record number of divorces. The divorce rate doubled from less than 2 divorces per 1000 Americans in the decades before World War II to 4.3 per 1000 people in 1946.[9] The divorce rate of 1946 remained unsurpassed until 1974. But even divorce could not stop the baby boom.

THE BOOM GOES ON

The soldiers started the baby boom, but what kept it going for nearly two decades has since puzzled demographers, sociologists, and economists. The second year of the baby boom was its most dramatic. In 1947, 1 million more babies were born than in 1945.[10] This spike in the age structure of the American population is still evident today. One million more people turned 40 in 1986, for example, than in 1985. If 40 is the age of mid-life crisis, then two decades of crisis have just begun.

From 1954 to 1964, over 4 million babies were born in the United States each year. (The peak year of the baby boom was in 1957, when 4.3 million babies were born.) But in 1965, the baby boom ended. Births fell to their lowest level since 1950. No one knows what stopped the baby boom, just as no one knows what sustained it for nearly two decades. Fashions changed and, like the hoola hoop, babies were on the out list. It may be more than coincidental, however, that the birth control pill became widely available to American women in 1963.

Since 1964, the annual number of births in the United States has never topped 4 million, despite the fact that there are more women of childbearing age alive now than ever before in history. If the women of childbearing age today were having as many children as their mothers did, more than 6 million Americans would be born each year.

By 1965, every American younger than age 20 was a baby boomer. In that year, however, no one identified the baby boom as a single generation. Americans did not know until the federal government published the vital statistics for 1965 that the birth boom was over, marking the end of the generation. And it took years of declining births for people to realize that the boom was not going to return. After nearly two decades of crowded maternity wards, the experts had thought that the American obsession with babies was a new way of life. Instead, it was only a 19-year upheaval of tradition.

Look magazine announced in 1965: "Fifteen years ago, the median age in the U.S. was 30.2 years. Today, it is 27.8 years. Fifteen years from now, it will be 25.5 years."[11] The magazine's editors did not know that the baby boom was over. By 1980 the median age of Americans was 30 and rising, as the number of American children declined.

Because of the few children each American woman is having, the median age of Americans should rise to 36 by the turn of the century.[12] Of course, this prediction may be just as inaccurate as the one *Look* magazine made more than 20 years ago, because no one knows how many children today's young women will have. But another baby boom is unlikely for several good reasons. First, the small families of the baby-boom generation represent a return to a longstanding American tradition. For 100 years, each succeeding generation of American women had fewer children, as more of their children survived to adulthood because of declining mortality rates. The women who gave birth to the baby-boom generation broke this historical pattern and had more children than their mothers did. Second, the educational level of American women is rising, and the more educated a woman is, the fewer children she has. Third, the American way of life has changed dramatically, making it difficult for women to have children and also provide their families with the money they now need to enjoy a middle-class lifestyle.

THE 1950s

The parents of the baby-boom generation grew up knowing hard times—the Depression and World War II. But they also knew the best of times. When they were young adults in the 1950s, the American economy boomed. The baby boom's parents married early, bought houses, and had babies. Jobs were plentiful and wages rose rapidly. Median family income increased by more than $5000 during the 1950s and by more than $6000 in the 1960s, even after adjusting for inflation.[13] In comparison, median family income did not increase at all during the 1970s, when the baby-boom generation came of age. Housing was inexpensive in the 1950s, enabling families to maintain a comfortable lifestyle on only one income.

The baby boom's parents had more money than they knew what to do with, says one theorist in explaining the baby boom, so they had babies. In the hard times of the 1930s, only 55% of women of childbearing age had two or more children. In the good times of the 1950s, 85% of women in the childbearing age group had at least two children.[14]

Richard A. Easterlin, a University of Southern California economics professor, formulated this theory during the 1950s as he saw the baby boom in progress. "As one of the baby boom parents myself, I came increasingly to feel, as a result of my work, that the history of my generation had been importantly affected by its scarcity," Easterlin writes in *Birth and Fortune*.[15] Easterlin's hypothesis is that small generations will do better economically than larger generations because of the laws of supply and demand. The baby boom's parents were members of the small generation born during the low-fertility years of the 1920s and 1930s. Because it was small, employers had to raise wages to attract workers. The baby boom's parents found themselves with fat paychecks. Because they were making more money than they expected, the parents of the baby boom felt free to marry and have children, devoting their excess income to toddlers, says Easterlin.

But not everyone agrees with Easterlin's theory about the cause of the baby boom. One troubling fact that counters his theory is that so many births during the baby-boom years were unwanted. The mothers of the baby-boom generation had more children than they planned to have because of sloppy contraception, say some demographers.[16] The baby boom's parents married young, half of them as teenagers. This placed them at risk of having unwanted children for more than two decades.

In 1965, married women reported that one-fifth of the babies they had had in the previous five years were unwanted.[17] If that proportion of unwanted births holds true throughout the baby boom years, then 16 million baby boomers were unwanted—a figure almost equal to the 17 million extra births that created the generation. As effective birth control became available in the 1960s, the proportion of births that were unwanted fell dramatically, to only 7% by 1982. In fact, the drop in fertility in the mid-1960s was due almost entirely to a reduction in unwanted births, according to demographer Leon F. Bouvier of The Population Reference Bureau.[18]

But American couples, despite imperfect birth control techniques, had managed to limit their family size before the baby-boom years. Why did couples fail to do so during the 1950s? The reason for their carelessness lies in the psychology of the times.

The allied victory in World War II gave Americans confidence in their institutions and leaders. The politicians and the military had achieved an enormous success, convincing Americans of the benevolence of authority—whether that authority was a politician, a minister, a psychiatrist, or a doctor.

"Americans today bear themselves like victory-addicted champions," said *Look* in 1965.[19] "They've won their wars and survived their depressions. They are accustomed to meeting, and beating, tests. They are experienced pragmatists, buoyed by a system that works. And they believe in their managers."

This trust in authority turned the 1950s into a decade of conformity. And it extended into the American home, defining the roles of husbands and wives. To have a successful marriage, the rules were clear: The husband must be the breadwinner and head of the family. The wife must be a full-time housewife and not challenge her husband's authority by earning her own paycheck. For women, this authoritarian family structure was a step backward from the new freedoms they had experienced in previous decades.

In 1947, *Life* magazine published "American Woman's Dilemma." In it, *Life* warned young housewives to think ahead, encouraging them to prepare for the future by going to work part-time while they were young so that they could later more easily fill the "free years after 40."[20]

Housework and child care alone are no longer interesting enough for a lifetime job, said *Life*. Instead, the magazine advised that when the housewife "finds really satisfying work to do she will discover that she is more interesting to her friends, to her husband and to herself."[21]

Less than a decade later, *Life* devoted a special issue to the American woman. In one article, five psychiatrists discussed the rules of a happy marriage and analyzed why some American marriages were not working out.

The problem, according to the psychiatrists, was "wives who are not feminine enough and husbands who are not truly male."[22]

Young married couples, they explained, suffered from sexual ambiguity. A good marriage, according to the psychiatrists, requires the husband and wife to follow strict rules regarding masculine and feminine behavior.

"If they are feminine women, with truly feminine attitudes, they will—without self-conscious exhortations about the delights of domesticity—accept their wifely functions with good humor and pleasure. They will not think of themselves as 'just a housewife.'"[23] Women who thought housework was dull, the psychiatrists warned, were rejecting their feminine role. And men, they said, should shoulder responsibility. They must give protection, not expect it.

The euphoria following World War II, the early marriages, the boom in births, and the belief in authority all made domesticity a fad and then the fashion of the times. For the millions of women bored with full-time cooking and cleaning, one more baby added interest to life. There was no need to control births carefully, since the families of the 1950s could afford to feed an extra mouth. The result was sloppy contraception.

It is no coincidence that the era of the feminine mystique and the years of the baby boom occurred simultaneously. Betty Friedan, who first attached a name to the fad of domesticity and childbearing in *The Feminine Mystique*, reports that "fulfillment as a woman had only one definition for American women after 1949—the housewife-mother."[24] The mystique grew through the 1950s. It held sway for about 15 years—not long in the overall scheme of things, but long enough to give birth to 76 million people.

Yet the cracks in the authoritarian world of the 1950s surfaced even at the zenith of the feminine mystique. Why else did men and women need to be told so often how to be men and women? "In 1956, at the peak of togetherness," Friedan reports, "the bored editors of *McCall's* ran a little article called 'The Mother Who Ran Away.' To their amazement, it brought the highest readership of any article they had ever run."[25] It struck a chord among the many mothers of the baby boomers who were unhappy with the narrow life the authorities had defined for them.

American women breathed a collective sigh of relief when they discovered in the pages of *The Feminine Mystique* that they were not alone in their lack of fulfillment, their feelings of boredom and even unhappiness. The era of the feminine mystique was over. But it gave birth to a special generation of Americans who rebelled against the way of life that had brought it into the world.

THE NEW WORLD

In the 1950s, the code word for conformity was "maturity," says social commentator Barbara Ehrenreich: "It is difficult, in the wake of the sixties' youth rebellion, to appreciate the weight and authority that once attached to the word 'maturity.'"[26]

According to the psychologists of the 1950s, the mature individual was one who had successfully completed eight developmental tasks: (1) selecting a mate, (2) learning to live with a marriage partner, (3) starting a family, (4) rearing children, (5) managing a home, (6) getting started in an occupation, (7) taking on civic responsibilities, and (8) finding a congenial social group.[27] Those who did not follow these rules were immature, which in the 1950s was synonymous with mentally ill.

As young adults, millions of baby boomers turned these rules upside down. They didn't select a mate and learn to live with a marriage partner; they lived with a succession of people outside of marriage. They didn't start families; they denounced bringing children into the world. They didn't manage homes; they lived in communes. They didn't get a job; they hitchhiked across the country. They didn't take on civic responsibilities—they fomented revolution. And the congenial social group of the baby boomers was decidedly uncongenial toward anyone aged 30 and older. The leading edge of the baby boom spurred a massive rebellion against authority.

It is not surprising that such a generation arose from the rigid world of the 1950s. First, the sheer numbers of baby boomers created a powerful teenage subculture. Businesses exploited the huge market, offering teens music and clothes that defied parental authority and the conformity of their parents' world. Second, the affluence of the 1950s gave young baby boomers the notion that just about everything was within their grasp. The proportion of American families with annual incomes of $25,000 or more rose from only 17% in 1952 to 53% in 1970 (after adjusting for inflation).[28] The acquisitive

American middle class rose to power. They in turn saw that the way to get ahead was to get an education. According to Fabian Linden, the director of The Conference Board's Consumer Research Center, education is the basis for Americans' social and economic mobility.[29] The parents of the baby boom are better educated than their parents, and the baby boom is even better educated than its parents.

Getting their children educated was the top goal of Americans in the 1960s, according to a Gallup survey.[30] Nearly nine out of ten baby boomers are high-school graduates, compared to two-thirds of their parents.[31] Half of baby boomers have been to college for at least one year, and one-fourth are college graduates. Only 14% of their parents graduated from college.[32] Baby-boom women have twice the college experience that their mothers have.

As this well-educated generation matured, it lifted the educational level of all Americans: In 1970, when the oldest baby boomer was just 24, only 55% of American adults had a high-school diploma. Today, 73% are high-school graduates.[33]

The baby-boom men born between 1947 and 1951 are the best educated people in American history. But it was the war in Vietnam, not a thirst for knowledge, that drove many inside the ivy-covered walls as they tried to avoid the draft, according to Census Bureau analysts.[34] Today, 28% of the men born between 1947 and 1951 have a college degree and 50% have at least one year of college. For men born since 1951, the proportions are slightly less. And there is still a difference in the proportion of men and women with a college diploma.

Until 1940, men and women were almost equally likely to go to college.[35] Between 1940 and 1970, as the feminine mystique took hold, men made significantly greater educational gains than women, creating a large gap in the percentage of men and women with a college degree. In 1970, 20% of men but only 13% of women aged 25 to 29 had graduated from college. The baby-boom women are closing this gap, however. By 1985, 23% of women and 25% of men aged 25 to 34 had been to college for four or more years.[36] Among their parents, only 10% of women compared to 19% of men have college diplomas.

Women earn half of all bachelor's degrees today, more than half of the master's degrees, and one-third of the doctorates. By the mid-1990s, women will earn half of the nation's doctorates too, according to projections by the National Center for Education Statistics.[37]

Nothing changes people so much as education. Education determines how they live, how they vote, what they buy, and what they believe. American society has become more diverse, and more accepting of diversity, because its members are more educated. This is why the baby boom forges new ways of life, and why there cannot be—no matter how much some people may want it—a return to the simple traditions of the past. Becoming educated makes life more complex because it turns black and white into shades of gray. Getting educated is like losing innocence—once lost, it is gone forever.

The more educated people are, the more interest they take in current events and the less afraid they are of ties with foreign countries.[38] The educated are more attached to new technologies, and more willing to experiment with new products and ways of buying things. College-educated people, for example, are more likely to buy products through the mail or use an 800 number than Americans in general. The educated are also more active in sports, more likely to go to museums and plays, and more involved in community events.

In many ways, the baby-boom generation is no different than previous generations: Nearly all baby boomers want to marry, and most want to have children. Three out of four baby boomers say that religion plays an important role in their lives; two out of three would welcome less emphasis on money, but three out of four do not want less emphasis on hard work. Family, religion, and work are important to most baby boomers, just as they are to most Americans.[39]

But the educational level of the baby boom creates important differences between it and older generations of Americans. These differences will not diminish with age, and they make it unlikely the baby boom will ever live like its parents did.

TWO GENERATIONS

Baby boomers are accountants in Boston, unemployed steelworkers in Pittsburgh, coal miners in West Virginia, ranchers in Wyoming, secretaries in Des Moines, and college professors in North Carolina. There are rich and poor baby boomers, gay and straight, black and white. In fact, the black baby boom was proportionately bigger than the white baby boom because the fertility of black women rose even more than that of white women during the baby-boom years, according to Leon F. Bouvier of the Population Reference Bureau.[40] Today, one in eight baby boomers is black—10 million people in all.

Perhaps the most important split within the baby-boom generation is between the younger boomers and the older ones. In general, the baby boomers born between 1946 and 1955 have a different outlook on life than those born between 1956 and 1964.

First, there are obvious differences. The older baby boomers are more likely to be married and to have children than the younger ones. Because they are older, they earn more money. Many of these differences will fade as the younger baby boomers get older. Other differences will remain, however, because the older boomers gained an advantage in life that the younger ones missed. The older ones got the best jobs and bought houses when prices were relatively low—all while the younger baby boomers were in high school and college.

After adjusting for inflation, real wages stopped growing in 1973—just when the younger boomers graduated from high school. Although the sluggish economy was hard on everyone, it hurt the younger baby boomers the most, according to economists Frank Levy and Richard C. Michel: "In a disastrous coincidence, these baby boomers were beginning their careers just as the economy went sour."[41]

Instead of looking forward to running the country someday, as their older brothers and sisters are doing, the younger baby boomers worry that they won't be able to find satisfying jobs, afford a home, or ever retire. The younger baby boomers are serious in their scramble for success because they fear that the older boomers stole their chances for the good life.

The average monthly mortgage payment for people who bought a home in 1979 is less than $450. For those who are buying a home today it approaches $900.[42] Though interest rates have fallen, housing prices have not. The baby boomers who bought houses before 1980 have hundreds of dollars a month more spending money, on average, than those who are buying homes today. The affluence of the older boomers will separate them from the younger ones for years to come. And it has created a split in the attitudes of older and younger baby boomers—the younger ones being much more serious about money, and much less serious about everything else.

In the fall of 1967, the baby boomers born in 1949 went to college. These freshmen were the first to be surveyed by the American Council on Education, which now surveys college freshmen every year. Comparing the results from 1967—when some of the oldest baby boomers were in college—with the results from 1982— when the youngest baby boomers were college freshmen—reveals the striking differences between the older and younger halves of the generation.

In 1967, only 44% of students said that an important objective was to be "very well off financially."[43] By 1982, fully 69% of students said that this was very important.[44] Eighty-three percent of students in 1967 said that "developing a philosophy of life" was very important. By 1982, only 47% thought having a philosophy of life was important.

Fifty-one percent of college freshmen in 1967 thought it was important to keep up with politics. By 1982, only 38% of freshmen wanted to keep up with politics. More important than politics to the younger ones is finding a way to make ends meet. Forty-three percent of the older baby boomers thought the disadvantaged deserved preferential treatment. Among the younger baby boomers, the proportion favoring such preferential treatment was only 36%. The younger baby boomers, struggling to make ends meet, aren't as likely to give the fellow over there a leg up when they feel mired in the mud themselves.

In a study of high-school seniors in 1972 (those born in 1954) and 1980 (those born in 1962), the National Center for Education Statistics found that the proportion of students in the academic track declined from 46% to only 38%.[45] The 1980 seniors were not as active in activities such as the school newspaper and yearbook; science, foreign language, and other academically oriented clubs; and student government. But 1980's high-school seniors participated more heavily in athletics, hobby clubs, vocational education clubs, drama, band, and chorus. The older half of the baby boom is more interested in intellectual and political pursuits than the younger half; it is more concerned about social causes and less worried about money.

"Overall, 1980 seniors assigned much more importance than 1972 seniors to work-related values and living close to parents and much less to correcting social and economic inequalities and to community leadership," said the Center.[46]

These differences may always separate the older baby boomers from the younger ones. Social commentator and author Daniel Yankelovich theorizes that the baby boom went through two periods of value change.[47] Between 1965 and 1975 (when the older baby boomers were teenagers and in college), young people rejected the established mores and rules of the 1950s. But beginning in the late 1970s, younger baby boomers rethought the rebellion of the older ones, which created two political generations.

Younger baby boomers are more hard-boiled than the older ones, according to Yankelovich, but they are just as permissive, if not more so, when it comes to individual rights and choices. Only 26% of 1982 college freshmen believe that married women should stay at home, for example, versus 57% of college freshmen in 1967 (most of the older boomers have since changed their minds about this).[48] Only 25% of the younger baby boomers favored banning a speaker from campus, versus 40% of their older brothers and sisters. Surprisingly, 21% of 1982 college freshmen had taken part in a campus demonstration, versus only 16% of the more radical college freshmen of 1967.

Though the baby boom is no monolith, it is united in its tolerance of diversity. The educational level of the baby boom makes it more accepting and even encouraging of individual differences and alternative lifestyles. The result is an increasingly diverse American culture in which single women have children through artificial insemination, avowed homosexuals run for public office, divorced parents have joint custody of their children, and people marry two or even three times without raising an eyebrow.

MIDDLE-AGED ANXIETIES

Most college-educated baby boomers believe that their generation is different from other generations living today, according to a Louis Harris poll.[49] Perhaps the baby boom believes it is unique because it succeeded in creating the world in its own image. What the generation demanded as teenagers it got as adults—a society ruled by diversity rather than conformity.

Though the baby boomers changed the world, nearly one-third of them are disappointed in their accomplishments. Twenty-nine percent of a nationally representative sample told *The New York Times* that they have accomplished less than they expected to when they were in high school.[50] In contrast, only 13% of people aged 40 to 64 said they had accomplished less than expected. Forty-seven percent of the older group said they had accomplished more than they expected, versus only 33% of baby boomers. These statistics might reflect the frustrations of impending middle age, or they could be more deeply rooted in the gap the baby boom sees between its potential and reality.

Because the generation is well educated, its sights are lifted. When the baby boomers went to college, nothing seemed impossible. They ended a war, got rid of a president, and changed the role of the individual in American society. Now, the humdrum realities of middle age are catching up to them—work, salaries, debts, children, lawns, cars. Many baby boomers fear that the days of endless possibility are over.

The baby boom will not grow old gracefully. Already, there are signs of hysteria. Despite aerobics, health clubs, home gymnasiums, and triathlons, Americans feel worse about their bodies today than they did in the early 1970s, according to a *Psychology Today* survey.[51] The reason for this drop in confidence is creeping age. Fifty-five percent of women report feeling unhappy with their weight, up from 48% in 1972. Among men, 41% are unhapppy today, up from 35% in 1972. Fully 20% of both men and women today are unhappy with the way their faces look, up from 8% and 11%, respectively, in 1972.

The middle-aged are typically the most unhappy with the way they look. Fewer than half of people aged 30 to 64 are satisfied with their weight, while most younger and older people say their weight is "about right" according to the National Center for Health Statistics.[52] The young have no reason to be unhappy with their bodies, and perhaps the old have given up. Fifty percent of 30- to 44-year-olds, and 55% of 45- to 64-year-olds, report that they are overweight. Four out of ten are trying to lose weight.

The baby boom's obsession with fitness is one of the consequences of its aging. Magazines such as *Superfit, Triathlete, Runner's World, Women's Sports and Fitness,* and *Bicycling* soothe the baby boom's fear of losing its looks and physical abilities as it gets older. But the most radical consequence of the aging of the baby boom is the rise in cosmetic surgery. Between 1981 and 1984, the number of cosmetic operations increased 61%. Plastic surgery is one of the fastest-growing medical specialties in the country, according to *New York* magazine. "It used to be that when people wanted to feel more confident, they'd go to a therapist, or to est. Now they're going to plastic surgeons," says writer Patricia Morrisroe.[53] Nearly half a million people had cosmetic surgery in 1984.

"You can have thin thighs in 30 days, but you can't look 30 if you're 40," says Morrisroe. "The first of the baby boomers are now middle-aged; they've already shown their enthusiasm for feel-good remedies, from drugs to est to Nautilus. Now they've discovered cosmetic surgery."[54] The boom in plastic surgery has only just begun.

Eventually every generation must accept the fact that it will not be young forever. The baby boomers face this now. Their fall from grace was dramatized recently in Coca Cola's decision to replace its original-formula Coke with a new version. Until the spring of 1985, the baby boom was the rope in the tug-of-war for market share between Coca Cola and Pepsi. Suddenly, the baby boomers became onlookers as the soft drink giants battled for the "new" generation—the teenage members of the so-called "baby-bust" generation that followed the baby boom.

Coca-Cola made its new Coke sweeter and less fizzy to appeal to teenagers. Within days of the announcement, Pepsi had a 15-year-old girl on network television making the switch to Pepsi. At that time, the youngest baby boomer was 21.

The real switch in the Cola Wars was not from old Coke to new Coke or from Coke to Pepsi, but from the baby boom to a younger generation. Teenagers drink more soft drinks than people in their 20s and 30s, so there was good reason for the soft drink companies to go after younger people. But the baby-bust generation is small, while the baby boom is huge. The Cola companies had forgotten about the giant generation that still controls the American market.

After the switch, consumers across the country bombarded Coca Cola with complaints; up to 1500 phone callers a day demanded that the company bring back the old Coke.[55] So, less than three months after announcing the introduction of new Coke, it brought back the old to quell consumer discontent. Now dubbed Coca Cola Classic, the old Coke is intended for the older market, says Bill Backer, who was once responsible for much of Coke's advertising and who now is president of the Backer & Spielvogel ad agency.[56] The new Coke, according to Backer, is for the kids. Within a year, Coke Classic was outselling new Coke by four to one.[57]

American businesses learned a lesson from the Coca Cola fiasco. Though youth was once the most important consumer market in the United States it no longer holds the power. Because of the middle-aging of the baby boom, older Americans now control the marketplace. But the baby boom also learned a lesson as it realized that it was no longer the new generation. Every generation discovers its own mortality. It took the baby boom longer than most to feel mortal because its enormous size filled the spotlight of youth for so long. But in only 15 years, half of the American population will be younger than the youngest baby boomer.

The baby boom generation may no longer be youthful. And many baby boomers may be disappointed in the realities of middle age. But in middle and old age, the baby boom will hold the reins of power more firmly in its hands than ever before.

MIDDLE AGE

CHAPTER 3

THE NEW RULES

In the 1950s men and women lived separate and dissimilar lives: the breadwinner husband and the homemaker wife. The baby boom changed that, creating new traditions and a new way of life. But the new traditions have rules that are just as rigid as those of the old ones. The most important rule is that it now takes two incomes to make ends meet.

Sixty-five percent of married couples younger than age 55 have two breadwinners today—husband and wife.[1] Those who follow this new rule will do well in the years ahead. Those who don't will fall behind.

In any decade, some people have an economic advantage over others because people's financial strength depends, in part, on how old they are. In the next two decades, many middle-aged baby boomers have a good shot at affluence.

Few baby boomers will earn exorbitant salaries, invent get-rich-quick technologies in their garages, or hit the jackpot in the state lottery. This isn't how most people make money. Instead, baby boomers will see their salaries rise as they get more on-the-job experience. And because both husband and wife will be earning peaking paychecks in the 1990s and 2000s, many baby boomers will find themselves well off.

Though small generations have an economic edge over large generations because a scarcity of workers drives wages up, the baby boom sidestepped the bad fortune of its large size by making the two-income family the rule. In the decades ahead, the affluent baby boomers will be those who are married.

Two incomes already make a big difference in the finances of the generation. The median household income of baby-boom couples was $35,000 in 1985 if the wife worked full time, $10,000 more than the median income of all baby-boom households.[2] If the wife worked part time, the couple's median household income was $29,000. If the wife did not work, it was only $24,000.

THE IMPORTANCE OF MARRIAGE

Most Americans have health insurance, and many have life insurance, disability insurance, and even mortgage insurance. But the best insurance for affluence is a marriage certificate. And the importance of marriage is growing.

Marriage is more important to a person's wallet than an education, job skills, or attitude toward work, according to a study by the University of Michigan's Institute for Social Research.[3] The Institute's Panel Study of Income Dynamics tracked a sample of 5000 familes for ten years and found that changes in income are linked more to marriage and divorce than to any individual skills or characteristics. Women are helped by marriage more than men, the researchers found, and they are hurt much more by divorce. As women earn more money, however, men are becoming increasingly dependent on their wives to help pay the bills.

In 1983, the wives in two-income couples earned 31% of their family's income.[4] Wives who worked full time contributed 41%. The wife's earnings keep most baby boomers' mortgage checks from bouncing each month. Sixty-nine percent of couples buying their first home in 1985 needed two incomes to afford the mortgage.[5]

Marriage has made a difference in the economic well-being of blacks for decades because black women have been more likely than white women to work. But blacks are much less likely than whites to be married, and this lowers their income statistics. The median income of black families is only 56% of the median income of white families because a large proportion of black families are headed by women, the poorest family type.[6]

The median income of black married couples is 78% of the median income of white married couples, according to the Census Bureau.[7] The median income of black couples in which the wife is employed full-time is fully 84% of the median income of two-earner white couples.

Marriage will polarize the lifestyles of the middle-aged in the next few decades, black and white: The married and remarried will be comfortable, and many will have money to spare; the single or divorced could find it hard to make ends meet because one person's income is no longer enough to pay for the most important trapping of a middle-class lifestyle—a home of one's own.

In 1963, the mortgage payment on a new home absorbed 19% of the median income of a man working full time. Today, the mortgage payment on a new home, even at a relatively low 10% interest rate, consumes 26% of the median income of a man working full time. Add on taxes, insurance, and utilities, and housing costs today absorb fully one-third of the median income of a working man.[8] Yet most banks won't give a mortgage to a family that must spend more than 28% of its income on housing.

The costs of home ownership hit the baby boom hard, but some boomers were hit harder than others, say Rutgers University housing experts George Sternlieb and James W. Hughes.[9] Millions of baby boomers boarded what they call the "housing train" before it left the station in the late 1970s; millions of others did not. The most affluent of the middle-aged in the decades ahead will be those who bought homes before prices soared. In most cases, these are the older baby boomers.

Nearly two-thirds of households headed by older baby boomers own their homes today; only one-third of the younger baby boomers own a home.[10] Those who bought houses in the 1970s now enjoy relatively low housing costs, and they already have substantial equity in their homes. Because it takes money to make money, the boomers who boarded the housing train can use their home equity to multiply their money for the rest of their lives. But for the baby boomers who are hanging onto their morgages by the skin of their two incomes, a divorce could mean that no one gets the house.

It may be unromantic to tie marriage and money so closely together. But love alone has proven to be a weak bond, easily broken. A century ago, life on the farm made marriage an economic necessity for men and women because it took the labor of both to run a farm efficiently. As men left the farm to work in offices and factories, however, marriage continued to be an economic necessity for women, but it was no longer economically important for men. Now that the two-income family is the norm, the baby-boom men are finding marriage to be an economic necessity just as their great-great-grandparents did. When the romance wears thin in the 1990s, husbands and wives may think twice before they go their separate ways. Divorce rates could decline.

When mortgage rates dropped sharply in 1986, many baby boomers took the plunge and became homeowners. Though home ownership rates among younger Americans fell in the past decade, the baby boom is likely to catch up if mortgage rates remain relatively low. Most Americans are willing to sacrifice for the biggest slice of the American dream. In ten years, three out of four baby boomers will be homeowners, but most will be able to afford it only with two incomes.

WORKING WOMEN

The baby boom did not invent the two-earner couple. Dual-earner married couples outnumbered single-earner couples as far back as 1969, when the first baby boomer was only 23.[11]

The baby boom did invent the working mother, however. In the past, women worked before they married, then dropped out of the labor force when they had children, returning to work when their children went to school at age 6 or left home at age 18. But nearly half of the women of the baby-boom generation are back at work by their child's first birthday.

Baby-boom women have many more opportunities in the work world than their mothers did. But their mothers had two advantages that baby-boom women don't have: the time to have children and the financial freedom to devote their days to raising them.

In 1970, only 24% of married women with children younger than age two worked; today, half of them have jobs. Among women with preschoolers, only one-third worked in 1970; the share today is 54%. Among women with children aged 6 to 17, fewer than half worked in 1970; 68% work today.[12]

Two out of three women who work have a full-time job—even the mothers of preschoolers.[13] This statistic reflects the opportunities and the frustration of the baby-boom women. While women don't want to give up what they've gained in the work world, many want to spend more time with their children. But their families can't afford it. Most women say that their families would suffer financially if they did not work, according to the 1985 Virginia Slims American Women's Poll.[14] This is the baby boom's dilemma.

Overall, more than half of American women work, comprising 44% of the nation's labor force. But among baby-boom women, fully 70% are in the labor force. According to projections by the Bureau of Labor Statistics, more than 80% will be working by 1995.[15]

Why have baby-boom women gone to work in such record proportions? Part of the answer may lie in the culture of the 1950s, which prescribed one role for all married women—homemaking. Many of the mothers of the baby boomers chafed at the narrowness of their lives. As their children matured, the daughters rejected the housewife role that had confined their mothers. Though women's participation rates in the labor force were on the rise long before the baby-boom women went to work—because of women's increasing levels of education and the growth of white-collar jobs in the American economy—the increase was slow until the baby-boom women came of age. Without the 1950s haunting them, baby-boom women might have drifted, rather than stampeded, into the workforce.

Once women went to work, they liked it. According to F. Thomas Juster of the University of Michigan's Institute for Social Research, the satisfaction men and women get from their jobs outranks what they get from most of their leisure activities.[16] Ranked in order of satisfaction, child care comes in first, followed by socializing, working, reading, participating in sports, attending spectator events, taking part in crafts, watching television, cooking, doing repairs, being a member of an organization, shopping, and—in last place—cleaning. Economists' projections of women's participation in the labor force are consistently too low, Juster suggests, because they fail to recognize the personal rewards that come with a job.

Women today are creating their own work traditions, and they are changing men as they do it. Most baby-boom men are married to working wives, and most working wives work full time.[17] The lives of baby-boom women and men are increasingly alike. Both go to work in the morning; both return home at the end of the day. This is a new twist on the traditional family.

In fact, the traditional family is not the breadwinner husband and the homemaker wife: That family was the norm only for the past century. "For all but a short period of human history, women have rivaled men in economic production," reports University of Southern California demographer Kingsley Davis.[18] When the United States was predominantly an agricultural country both men and women worked at home on the farm. Men produced the crops while women produced in the home—they raised and educated children, grew and preserved food, prepared meals, cleaned and fueled lights, stoked ovens and stoves, emptied slop buckets, and manufactured clothes and cleaned them. By 1920, however, many of their chores were done outside the home by businesses—lighting, heating, plumbing, prepared foods, and store-bought clothes became available to the majority of families early in this century. Such conveniences eclipsed the housewife's economic role in the family. If women had insisted on continuing to do these tasks, they would have gone to work a century ago as plumbers, utility foremen, food and clothing manufacturers, laundry operators, and school administrators. Instead, women remained at home, but it was only a matter of time before they would go back to work.

The breadwinner family system is associated with a particular stage of economic development, says demographer Davis. It makes women economically dependent on men, but it frees men of their dependence on women. Today, the United States economy is evolving beyond the breadwinner system. Men and women are dependent on one another once again.

According to estimates by the Bureau of Labor Statistics, men aged 25 in 1980 could expect to work for 33 years, women for 24 years.[19] While men's work life expectancy has not changed since 1970, women's has risen by five years as increasing numbers of women have gone to work. And for women aged 25 with at least some college education, the expected work life is fully 28 years—enough to earn them a gold watch—and not far behind the 36 years of work life expected for college-educated men.

The working woman has changed the nation's businesses, government, schools, and homes. The full impact of the working woman will be played out in the 1990s and the first decades of the next century, when women who are just now earning their degrees in business, medicine, law, dentistry, physics, engineering, and other professions will be firmly entrenched in their careers. Only 5% of the nation's lawyers were women in 1970; 20% are today.[20] By early in the next century, one-third of the nation's lawyers, business executives, and doctors will be women.

The two-earner family system will raise women's earnings relative to men's. It will change American institutions that have long regarded men and women as separate and unequal. It will pressure the politicians to create laws that allow employees to combine work and family responsibilities more easily. It may even influence our foreign policy, as the United States encourages other countries to treat men and women as equals.

THE BABY-BOOM LABOR FORCE

Half of current American workers were born since 1950. During the 1970s, the number of young workers grew rapidly as the baby-boom generation flooded the labor force. In the 1990s, the number of middle-aged workers will grow rapidly as the boom generation celebrates more birthdays.

The aging of the baby boom should help to raise the productivity of American workers because the longer workers are on the job, the more productive they are. It also should help to lower the unemployment rate. As the number of young people looking for work declines in the decade ahead, entry-level job opportunities and pay should increase. The maturing of the baby boom into the prime working years should keep the unemployment rate down for years—until the baby boom's own children compete with each other for jobs.

Today, one-fourth of American workers are college graduates. The labor force participation rate of men does not vary much by educational level, but for women an education makes a dramatic difference. Fully 78% of women aged 25 to 64 who are college graduates are in the labor force, versus 64% of women who went no further than high school.[21]

The well-educated baby-boom generation is upgrading many jobs. Those that once required a high school diploma now ask for a college degree. As this happens, the work world is becoming more complex. Computer analysts, media consultants, market researchers, historic preservationists, landscape architects, meteorologists— colleges created these educated specialists. And the specialists create new kinds of work.

Through 1995, the Bureau of Labor Statistics projects that the biggest percentage gains in number of workers will be in jobs that require a college degree, such as electrical engineering, computer science, physical therapy, law, and accounting. But the jobs that will gain the most workers in absolute numbers during the next decade are cashiers, registered nurses, janitors, truck drivers, waiters and waitresses, salesworkers, and nursing aides, most of which do not require much schooling.[22]

The Bureau of Labor Statistics also projects that some jobs will become scarce in the next few decades. Baby boomers who work in farming or on the railroad; those who are stenographers, college professors, or postal service clerks; or those who run sewing machines for a living may find themselves out of work. But the boomers who devoted years to getting their Ph.D.s and who ended up driving taxis and pumping gas will find the job situation easing in the mid-1990s when the baby boom's children reach college age. College administrators already worry about a possible shortage of teachers ten years from now.

WHAT BABY BOOMERS DO

Few baby boomers wear three-piece suits or carry briefcases. Only 9% of working baby-boom men and 6% of working baby-boom women are business executives. Another 10% of men and 12% of women work in the professions, such as nursing, teaching, law, medicine, and architecture.[23]

Yet despite all the talk about the young, urban professional, the largest share of baby-boom men (18%) are blue-collar workers in precision production, craft, and repair occupations: machinists, cabinetmakers, bakers, tool and die makers, and the like. The largest share of baby-boom women (22%) are clerks and secretaries.

Twenty years from now, when the baby boom nears retirement, most will work in the same occupations as they do today. Though people work at an average of ten different jobs during their lives, they are most likely to change jobs when they are young. By age 24, according to economist Robert E. Hall, workers have held four of their ten jobs. The next 15 years contribute another four.[24]

Overall, American men have been working at their current jobs a median of 4 years, down from 5.7 years in 1963, according to the Employee Benefit Research Institute.[25] Women have been at their current jobs a median of only 1.5 years, down from 3 years in 1963. This decline in overall job tenure is due, in large part, to the influx of young workers into the labor force in the past 20 years.

Among men aged 45 to 54, job tenure is down only slightly, from 11.4 years in 1963 to 11 years in 1981. In 1951, job tenure for men in this age group was only 7.6 years. Men aged 35 to 44 have been at the same job a median of 6.6 years, down from 7.6 years in 1963.

Job tenure for women aged 45 to 54 has fallen from a median of 6.1 years in 1962 to 5.1 years, but it remains above the 4-year median of 1951. Women aged 35 to 44 have been at the same job a median of 3.5 years.

When people change jobs, they usually stay in the same line of work. But young adults often change careers as well. Each year, one in five people aged 20 to 24 changes careers.[26] Waitresses become secretaries; truck drivers become factory workers. Only 12% of people aged 25 to 34 and 7% of 35- to 44-year-olds change careers in a year. Overall, Americans can expect to change careers three time in their lives.

In middle age, many baby boomers will turn their jobs into a career. Among 30- to 44-year-olds, 58% regard their work as a career.[27] That's what all the job hopping is about—finding a better salary, a better job title, and ultimately finding work that offers more than a paycheck.

WHAT BABY BOOMERS WILL EARN

In the 1980s, the baby boomers discovered that money matters. It determines their lifestyle and defines their friendships. High-school friends, for example, may no longer have much in common because one person has money and the other doesn't. One person travels to the Caribbean every February; the other can't pay the electric bill. One owns a big house, the other lives in a mobile home.

For some baby boomers, the money that defines their lives is a matter of choice—they spent years in school earning degrees and now they get the rewards. The median income of all baby-boom households was $25,000 in 1985, but for those headed by college graduates, it was fully $34,000.[28] College-educated men aged 25 to 34 earn 39% more than men aged 25 to 34 who went no further than high school, according to the Census Bureau.[29] The one in four baby boomers who have a college diploma are likely to reap its benefits for the rest of their lives.

College degree or not, the incomes of most baby boomers will never be much to brag about, especially compared to what their fathers made. Between 1950 and 1960, men's median income rose 29% (after adjusting for inflation).[30] In the 1960s, it rose another 25%. The average man was making nearly $7000 more in 1970 than in 1950—that's on top of inflationary increases in pay. Since 1970, however, men's median income has fallen 13% after adjusting for inflation, in part because the baby boom crowded into the labor force and lowered wages,

but also because of the high inflation in the late 1970s
and early 1980s.

Baby boomers are more likely to make a little money
than a lot. Nearly one-third of baby-boom men and over
half of baby-boom women make less than $10,000 a
year.[31] Among baby-boom households, one in seven
has an income below $10,000.[32] By 1995, only one in ten
will have an income that low (in 1985 dollars), according to Wharton Econometric Forecasting Associates.[33]
Though it's hard to believe, an income of $10,000 a year
is well above the poverty threshold for a person who
lives alone (poverty threshold: $5600) or for a family of
two ($7200) or three ($8600). Only for a family of four
does $10,000 fall below the poverty line of $11,000.

Nine percent of baby-boom men and 14% of baby-
boom women live in poverty.[34] But 24% of black baby
boomers are poor, and so are 23% of Hispanics. Only 8%
of married couples are poor, but over half of the baby-
boom women who head families alone live in poverty.

Many baby boomers went to work when jobs were
hard to find, when pay eroded rapidly because of inflation, when divorce meant more women were raising children alone, and when government benefits to children
fell. Nevertheless, most baby boomers believe they are
doing well. In fact, 74% of baby-boom men and 70% of
baby-boom women say they are as well off as or better off
than their parents were when they left their parents'
homes, according to a survey by The Conference
Board.[35] Perhaps that's because a majority of baby
boomers believe they have more opportunities than their
parents. Seventy-six percent of baby-boom men and 88%

of baby-boom women say they have more opportunity than their fathers or mothers had at their age.

Though most baby boomers think they are better off than their parents, those at the top of the income scale are a tiny minority. Only 4 in 100 men and 6 in 1000 women personally make more than $50,000 a year. But one in nine baby-boom households had an income above $50,000 in 1985.[36] The boost that marriage gives to income is clear. Baby-boom couples have a median household income nearly three time higher than that of the unlucky women who are raising children alone.

Baby-boom men who worked full time had a median personal income of $22,000 in 1985. Baby-boom women who worked full time had a median personal income of just $16,000.[37]

Men who are executives, administrators, and managers make the most money, a median weekly income before taxes of $614, versus only $416 a week for all men who worked full time in 1986.[38] Ranking second on the income scale are men in the professions—doctors, dentists, lawyers, and so on—with a weekly income of $596.

Close to the median for all men are blue-collar workers—men in the precision production, craft, and repair occupations—with weekly earnings of $418. On the low end of the scale are laborers (making $272) and farmers ($220).

The highest-paid women are mechanics and repairers, earning $438 a week—far below the earnings of the highest-paid men, but more than the $417 a week earned by male mechanics and repairers. Women in the professions earn a weekly paycheck of $424, compared to only $290 a week on average for all women who work full time. Women executives and managers make $401 a week. Women working as clerks and secretaries make only $281 a week. The lowest-paid women are maids, cooks, and housecleaners, earning only $118 a week.

No matter what their occupation, most baby boomers can look forward to rising incomes in their middle age because people make more as they get older and gain work experience. Men's earnings peak when they are in their 40s and 50s, then their earnings fall as they retire. Right now the statistics show hardly any peak in women's earnings by age. But this is a statistical fluke, because many older women workers are in traditional female jobs that don't pay much, while younger women have not been on the job long enough to be making top dollar. As the career-minded women of the baby-boom generation get older, they will raise the incomes of all women and close some of the gap between men's and women's earnings.

For highly educated women, income does increase with age.[39] Among full-time working women who have been to graduate school, those aged 25 to 34 made $21,000 a year in 1984. Those aged 45 to 54 made $28,000, and women aged 55 to 64 made close to $30,000.

WOMEN BREADWINNERS

Sex discrimination is only one of the reasons that women earn less than men. The other reasons include, first, the fact that men are better educated than women. The higher a person's education, the higher the income. Second, the average woman worker has not been on the job as long as the average male worker. Employers reward workers for length of service. Third, women are more likely than men to drop out of the labor force when they have children. These gaps in employment lower women's pay.

Women's earnings as a percentage of men's have been fairly stable for years, ranging from 61% in 1960 to 64% today.[40] But the ratio should rise in the next two decades as the ambitious women of the baby-boom generation gain in job experience and seniority. By 2000, according to projections by the Rand Corporation, working women should be earning 74% of what working men earn.[41]

Though most women make less money than men, a growing proportion of wives make more than their husbands. The wife is the main breadwinner for nearly one-fifth of the nation's 26 million two-income couples.[42] An additional 2 million wives earn 80% to 100% of what their husbands earn, bringing the share of wives who earn at least 80% of what their husbands earn to 27%. These top-earning wives are more likely than other wives to have a college degree and to be professionals or managers, according to the Census Bureau.

The number of women who earn more than their husbands is increasing as the baby boom inflates the number of working women and working wives. In 1974, only 9% of wives earned more than their husbands. By 1981, the proportion was 12%, and in 1983 (the latest year for which statistics are available) it was 18%.[43]

For some of these couples, this financial arrangement is temporary—the husband is unemployed for a few months and in the meantime the wife supports the family. But for other couples, the wife is likely to make more than her husband throughout her life because she is better educated or her line of work pays more. Only about half of the wives who earn more than their husbands are likely to do so for life, according to Census Bureau demographer Suzanne Bianchi.

What impact does this have on a marriage? The findings are mixed. If the family expects the husband to be the primary breadwinner and he is not, the couple could be headed for divorce court. But if husband and wife have no strong preferences about which one should earn more, then the marriage should be as stable as any, according to Bianchi.

As increasing numbers of wives become their family's primary breadwinner, this role reversal will be easier for men and women to accept. Already, most Americans feel comfortable with the idea of a wife earning more than a husband. Surprisingly, men accept it more than women. According to the 1985 Virginia Slims American Women's Poll, 74% of men said they would be perfectly comfortable if their wives earned more than they did.[44] Sixty-eight percent of women—a majority, but a smaller one than among men—said they would feel perfectly comfortable earning more than their husbands.

The chances will never be fifty–fifty that a wife outearns her husband, however. Biology intervenes, making women's priorities different from men's. As long as women bear children, statistics will show that, on average, wives earn less than their husbands. For some women, children will be more important than a paycheck.

PEAK EARNINGS

Most Americans believe they are in the middle class. Few people are willing to admit that they fall into the lower class, and not too many feel rich enough to place themselves in the upper class. But in a study of Americans' incomes, economist Stephen J. Rose draws the lines, defining the classes.[45] The middle class, he says, had a household income that fell between $19,000 and $47,000 in 1986.

In recent years, the middle class has been shrinking, says Rose. In 1978, 52% of American households were middle class. By 1986, only 44% were. The lower class captured some of the middle class, growing by five percentage points since 1978, to 34% of all households. The upper class also absorbed some of the middle class, increasing by three percentage points since 1978 to 22% of all households.

The increase in the lower class, says Rose, is the fault of divorce. "When a husband and wife separate, the same income may exist, but the costs are greater—two rents must be paid, two homes furnished and heated."[46] But when the divorced fall into the lower class, their stay is usually temporary. Upon remarriage, most of them are back in the middle class, and many of them climb into the upper class, especially if they have two incomes. Since 1978, says Rose, the rise in the upper class has been due in large part to the increase in two-income couples.

Most baby boomers have middle- or lower-class incomes today. But in the decades ahead, a growing proportion will find themselves in the upper class.

The median income of a baby-boom man who works full time was $22,000 in 1985. When his earnings peak, this man can expect to make a median of around $30,000 a year (in 1985 dollars). Today, a baby-boom woman who works full time makes a median of $16,000 a year. Her earnings are likely to peak at between $20,000 and $25,000 a year (in 1985 dollars). If this man and woman are husband and wife, their household income will peak at more than $50,000 a year.

Of course these statistics are national averages. There are regional and local differences in earnings across the country because it costs more to live in some places than in others. In New England and the Pacific Coast, median incomes are higher than average; in the South, they are below average. Baby boomers in metropolitan areas such as New York, Boston, and San Francisco will make more than those in Des Moines or Kansas City. But the cost of living in New York or San Francisco absorbs any extra money that people there make. A 2000-square-foot, four-bedroom home that costs $74,000 in Columbus, Ohio, for example, would cost $375,000 in San Francisco and a whopping $600,000 in Greenwich, Connecticut, according to a Coldwell Banker survey.[47] This means that a person living in San Francisco needs to make five times as much money as someone living in Columbus, Ohio just to stay even.

Yet affluence is a state of mind more than a bank account. Some people can be rich on $15,000 a year; others not even on $100,000. Where people live, their family size, and how much their homes cost all determine how affluent they feel.

Affluence once meant a household income of $30,000 or more. Today, a large proportion of baby-boom households—more than one-third—have achieved that level of affluence. By 1995, over half of baby-boom households will have an annual income of $30,000 or more (in 1985 dollars), according to Wharton Econometric Forecasting Associates.[48] But most families with incomes of $30,000 a year aren't rich. In a study of these households, economist Courtenay Slater finds that only a fraction of them are wealthy.[49] Most have two or more workers, a home with a mortgage, a checking and a savings account, and a net worth of $78,000, she says.

The New York research firm FIND/SVP defined the affluent as households with incomes of $40,000 and over.[50] At this cut-off, about one in five baby-boom households is affluent. Most households with incomes of $40,000 or more are headed by college-educated, two-income, married couples, says FIND/SVP. Two out of three of these "affluent" households do not have any members who alone make as much as $40,000. For most households, it takes two incomes to achieve affluence.

Today, about 10% of baby-boom households have annual incomes of $50,000 or more. In ten years, one-fourth will have incomes that high (after adjusting for inflation).[51] The characteristics of the households with incomes of $50,000 plus are familiar—married couples, two incomes, well educated, raising children.

Only 2% of households headed by baby boomers have incomes of $75,000 or more, according to the Census Bureau.[52] But in 1995, 7% of baby-boom households will have an income of $75,000 plus (after adjusting for inflation).[53] And in 2005, 10% of baby-boom households will be in this income elite, according to Wharton projections.[54]

Those who won't be satisfied with anything less than a million should take heart. Many will make a million. A baby-boom man with a college education will make $1.3 million in a lifetime of full-time work.[55] Those with high-school diplomas will make $954,000 in their lives. A baby-boom woman with a college education who works full time will make $772,000 in her lifetime, and if she went to graduate school she'll make $900,000. Yet, considering that it costs over $100,000 to raise one child—and that doesn't include college tuition—the baby boomers may not have much to show for a lifetime of work. Though most will own a home, few will own a second home. Though most will buy a new car every few years, few will drive a Mercedes.

FRINGE BENEFITS

Fringe benefits are an important part of today's jobs. The fringes will be getting sweeter in the next few decades because benefit packages designed for the family of the 1950s are being redesigned for the individual of the 1980s.

The traditional fringe benefit package is now obsolete, according to economists David E. Bloom and

Michael P. Martin.[56] Employers once offered their workers a single benefit package, take it or leave it. In the years ahead, however, most companies will offer their employees a choice of benefits to keep disgruntled baby boomers on the job.

The baby boom is aging into a middle manager squeeze. By the turn of the century, the number of highly qualified baby boomers ready for top management positions will outnumber the top-ranking positions available. Millions of baby boomers will find themselves plateaued in middle age. For the achievers, this means disappointment unless they can pursue other ways to get ahead. But, even stalled at middle age, the baby boomers will be valuable to their companies because there's no one to replace them. The scarcity of workers in the next (baby-bust) generation makes the baby boom valuable, and powerful. Employers will have to offer them alternatives, such as attractive fringe benefits, to keep them on the job.

If there's no room at the top, will an extra few weeks of vacation make up for it? Maybe so. Market researcher Judith Langer has identified a new attitude among people in their 30s and 40s that she calls "backing off workaholism."[57] Some ambitious professionals, she says, are opting for less demanding jobs and more flexible work schedules in order to have more time for relationships and personal interests. Because the baby boom takes its leisure seriously, companies may be surprised at how eagerly it accepts flexible schedules and more free time in exchange for staying on the job and feeling good about it.

As the baby boom moves into management positions, it will create more flexible job benefit policies, says Helen Axel, director of the Conference Board's Work and Family Information Center.[58] Workers covered by their spouse's health insurance plan should be able to pass up their own company's health insurance, for example, and opt for extra vacation time instead. They should be able to pick dental insurance instead of life insurance. Or they could choose child care benefits instead of vacation time. The service industries, like publishing, advertising, and health care, will be the first to adopt flexible plans since they are growing rapidly and need to attract employees. The old-line industries dominated by male workers, such as mining and manufacturing, will be the last to change.

One benefit that baby boomers will demand in the 1990s is child care. In 1986, about 2500 United States companies offered their employees child care benefits (such as on-site day care centers, flex-time, and direct financial assistance). This is four times the number of companies that did so only four years earlier, according to the *Harvard Business Review*.[59] But the number of businesses that offer child care services is small in comparison to the tens of thousands that don't. In fact, only 1% of employees in the nation's medium-sized and large firms have child care benefits available to them, according to the Bureau of Labor Statistics.[60]

One reason more companies don't offer child care benefits is that they don't know how much the baby boom needs them. Many top business executives think most of their employees live in traditional families, with a wife at home to take care of the kids, says Dana E.

Friedman in the *Harvard Business Review*. But in fact only a minority of workers live in this type of family today.

Other corporate executives don't realize that the rules have changed. Their philosophy is that if the wife isn't at home with the kids, she should be. But baby-boom women can't afford to stay home. Among working women with children under age 6, 29% have a relative caring for their children while they're at work, and 44% have their children in a nursery school or a day care center, or with a babysitter, a friend, or a neighbor. The fathers care for another 20% while their wives are at work.[61]

Despite the difficulty in juggling work and children, 78% of working mothers say they are very satisfied with their child care arrangements, according to the Virginia Slims poll. But fully eight out of ten Americans want more day care centers. Most parents manage to find a satisfactory solution to their child care problems, but they want more choice.

Will private companies or the federal government meet this demand, offering comprehensive care for children and generous leave for parents? The United States is one of the few developed countries in the world that does not guarantee some kind of maternity leave for its pregnant workers. If this indifference is ever going to disappear, it will happen in the next 15 years, when a huge proportion of Americans face the child care problem. But for most baby boomers, the need for day care lasts only a few years. As soon as a family's children are in school, its day care needs drop sharply. This creates a rapid turnover in the constituency favoring expanded services, weakening the public support for child care benefits.

Another job benefit that workers will pay more attention to in the next decade is the company pension plan. Many baby boomers do not believe Social Security will afford them much of a retirement income, and most workers cannot save enough money to support themselves comfortably in retirement. Even workers who manage to save a whopping 20% of their income every year for 40 years will provide themselves with only 40% of their annual preretirement income during 20 years of retirement, according to an analysis by the Employee Benefit Research Institute (EBRI).[62] Pension experts estimate that retirees need 60% to 70% of their annual preretirement income to live comfortably. This makes pensions an important benefit—perhaps the most important job benefit after health insurance.

Most baby boomers will need a company pension to boost their retirement income. Yet only 51% of all full-time wage and salary workers covered by a pension plan are currently "vested" in the plan—meaning they are entitled to receive money from their employer upon retirement.[63] Until recently, it took ten years of service to become fully vested in most company pension plans. Because baby boomers are in the ages of job hopping, few qualified for company pensions—nine out of ten have been with their current employer for less than ten years. But the Tax Reform Act of 1986 lowered pension vesting from ten years to five. The EBRI estimates that this change will greatly increase the proportion of baby-boom households that eventually receive a company

pension, from 63% under the ten-year vesting provisions
to 81%. But some companies may not be able to afford
five-year vesting, and they may drop their pension
benefits altogether.

"Too few workers know enough about their retirement needs or about their retirement benefits in their
current jobs or prospective jobs to make intelligent de-
cisions about changing companies," notes *The Wall Street
Journal*.[64] Baby boomers who consider a job change
should compare carefully the pension benefits they give
up with those they get.

SELF-EMPLOYMENT

Some people won't feel good about being trapped
in middle management no matter how much vacation
time or pension income their company offers them.
These baby boomers are likely to strike out on their own.
Today, 10 million Americans are self-employed, about
one in ten workers. One-third of the self-employed are
women.[65]

Until the 1970s, the ranks of the self-employed were
shrinking because of the long-term decline in the number of farmers in the United States.[66] But nonagricul-
tural self-employment began to grow rapidly in the
1970s, reversing the decline.

Most of the self-employed do not make much
money, however. Women who worked full time at self-
employment earned $6000 in 1982. This was just half the
median earnings of women who worked full time at

wage-and-salary jobs. Men who worked full time at self-employment had median earnings of $14,400 in 1982, only two-thirds of what men working full time as wage-and-salary workers earned. Yet self-employed workers work longer weeks than wage-and-salary workers—an average of 40 hours for the self-employed versus 38 for wage-and-salary workers. (Of course, the apparently lower earnings of the self-employed may be due in part to the fact that the self-employed are more likely than wage-and-salary workers to have unreported income.)

Though it may mean more work for less pay, self-employment has a certain glamour to it, and it is likely to become more common. The two-income family encourages experimentation with self-employment because one spouse can strike out on his or her own while the other shoulders the family's financial burden for a while. But the baby boomers who cut the cord and devote all their working hours to their own businesses risk poverty when they are too old to work. The self-employed do not get the job benefits that employees get, particularly a company pension. Unless these entrepreneurs are careful about putting a considerable portion of their income away in a retirement account, they risk being dependent only on Social Security in old age, or on their spouse's pension plan.

Despite these drawbacks, millions of baby boomers are likely to dabble in self-employment in the decades ahead from the safety of a 9-to-5 job. Some of these part-time businesses may last only a few years. But others will succeed, becoming new American corporations.

CHAPTER 4

THE NEW HOMEMAKERS

The middle-aging of the baby boom is turning the United States into a nation of homebodies. For the next two decades the home will be the focus of American life. But the home isn't what it used to be—Mom, Dad, and the kids have formed an intricate web of relationships because of the baby boom's complex lives.

John and Martha, born in the 1950s, met in college. They lived together for two years, then they married. Four years later they had a baby. John and Martha separated when their child was three, looking for greener pastures elsewhere. Martha, who had custody of the child, soon remarried. John lived by himself until he met

a woman who had two children from a previous marriage. They moved in together, then married. John and
Martha, two baby boomers in their 30s, now appear to
be living in traditional nuclear families—mother, father,
and children. But appearances can deceive. Scratch the
surface calm and divorce, stepchildren, stepparents, ex-
husbands, ex-wives, and a host of emotional and financial arrangements emerge.

Three out of four households headed by baby
boomers are families—which the Census Bureau defines
as a group of people related through blood, marriage, or
adoption. Over half of households headed by baby
boomers are married couples. But these statistics mask
the generation's complex family ties, hiding the flux in
baby-boom lives.

THE IMPOSSIBLE DREAM

No one can control the course of life completely.
Though most baby boomers long for a perfect family,
their chances of achieving this goal without some com-
promises and disappointments along the way are slim.
One demographer has calculated how slim. In a study
of what the chances are that newlyweds will achieve
their ideal family, John Bongaarts of the Population
Council examined the probability of upsets occurring in
two decades of marriage.[1]

Bongaarts's hypothetical couple marries when the
wife is 25 years old. The couple wants two healthy children, one boy and one girl, spaced three years apart.

Though these goals are modest, the probability that the couple will achieve them is a minuscule 6%.

This is because all sorts of things can—and do—get in the way. For the hypothetical couple, there are many obstacles: contraceptive failure (probability, 13%), involuntary childlessness (6%), miscarriage (20%), birth defects (2%), having two children of the same sex (50%), having an unwanted birth (30%), divorcing within 20 years (43%), and the death of a child or parent (4% and 9%, respectively). If only 6 in 100 couples can achieve the ideal family, then most baby boomers must learn to be happy with less.

By 1995, two-thirds of households headed by baby boomers will be married couples. Eighty percent of these couples will be raising children. The baby boom will be the establishment. From the outside, the baby boomers will look like they are following traditions laid down by their parents and grandparents. From the inside, however, nothing will be exactly as it used to be.

TEMPORARY LIFESTYLES

Typically, people leave their parents' home and then marry; they live with their spouse, have children, and become a nuclear family; the children grow up and the parents become empty nesters. One spouse dies and the survivor lives alone. This is called the lifecycle.

In the past, people followed the lifecycle from beginning to end, usually without interruption. Today, the baby boom is upsetting the lifecycle. Because of cohabitation, delayed childbearing, divorce, and remarriage, many baby boomers are stepping out of the cycle, resetting it, and starting over again.

A study by the Rand Corporation shows how temporary living arrangements can be.[2] In a study of American households, Rand researchers calculated how long different living arrangements last, on average. The most temporary lifestyle is cohabitation—people of the opposite sex living together outside of marriage. Half of these households break up within 1.8 years.

One reason these households change is that lovers get married. But this lifestyle doesn't last long either. The Rand researchers found that married-couple households last a median of 4.2 years before they become something else—because a couple divorces or has a child and becomes a nuclear family.

The nuclear family is the most stable household type. Even so, it lasts only a median of 6.9 years, say the researchers.

Though people marry thinking that it is forever, for most baby boomers it isn't. Many people (especially women) soon find themselves raising a child alone. Single-parent families last a median of 3.9 years before the parent remarries or the children are on their own, leaving the parent alone.

People live alone a median of 4.8 years before their living arrangement changes again (they remarry or they get a roommate, or they die), the Rand researchers found.

THE UNMARRIED

Most baby boomers have already married at least once, but they waited a long time to tie the knot. The baby boom is famous for its singleness. But the generation is breaking little new ground as it waits to pair off—today's singleness is a return to the marriage patterns that held sway early in this century.

In 1985, 59% of women in their early 20s were single, up from 36% in 1970.[3] One-fourth of women in their late 20s have never married, up from 11% in 1970. Women in their early 30s are twice as likely to be single today as women in that age group were in 1970.

It's not today's statistics that are so unusual, however. Instead, the statistics from 1970 are skewed by the marriage patterns of the 1950s. Half of first-time brides in the 1950s were teenagers. Little wonder that by 1970, the proportion never married among women in their early 30s had reached rock bottom.

Because people can marry at almost any age, it's difficult to identify people who will never marry. In analyzing such trends, demographers usually look at rates of singlehood for people aged 45 to 54 because by that age those who remain unmarried are unlikely to ever marry. "Using this criterion," says Cornell professor Edward L. Kain, "singlehood is not on the rise at all."[4]

According to Kain, "Young Americans are returning to levels of singlehood that have been characteristic throughout the history of this country—but which were interrupted by a few decades of unusually high marriage rates and low ages at marriages."[5]

A century ago, 52% of women aged 20 to 24 were unmarried—a proportion barely surpassed today. Twenty-five percent of women aged 25 to 29 had not married in 1890—again about equal to the share of baby-boom women in that age group who are still single.

But these facts do not deter the nation's media from sensationalizing the singleness of baby boomers. In one study of the chances of marriage for today's college-educated women, demographers estimated that only 20% of single women aged 30 will ever marry.[6] Among those aged 35, only 5% will marry. But these statistics are not as grim as they sound. First, some of these single women are living with men; second, many of these women don't want to marry.

"Many women today are unwilling to make the sacrifices that many men are still asking of them, and these are sacrifices that the men themselves would never agree to," comments Yale sociologist Neil Bennett, an author of the study.[7]

Most single women younger than age 30 are happy in their unwedded state. A 1983 study of unmarried women found that only 26% of single women in their 20s expected to marry and wished they already were.[8] Only 1% of single women in their 20s wanted to marry but didn't think they ever would. That left fully 73% of single women who were happy about being single. Of course many of these women may decide being single is not so much fun if they still haven't found Mr. Right in a few years, and most will marry. Demographer Paul C. Glick of Arizona State University projects that just 10% of baby-boom men and 12% of baby-boom women will never marry.[9]

Only 1% of baby boomers believe that being single is the ideal lifestyle, according to the Virginia Slims American Women's Opinion Poll.[10] Nevertheless, singles are happier than people think; even those who live by themselves aren't lined up at the lonely hearts club.

In an investigation of the quality of life of people who live alone, researchers from the Institute for Social Research at the University of Michigan examine how much contact single people have with friends, relatives, and neighbors. They find that "unmarried persons show many more visible signs of an active extra-household social life than is true for the married."[11] They conclude that "living alone appears to be an arrangement of choice in many cases, and it is not necessarily a catastrophic situation into which persons are forced against their will."

UNMARRIED MOTHERS

For women, being single does not mean what it once did. Single women today can make a good income, travel freely, and have an active sex life. They can even do something that the so-called spinsters of a century ago could not even imagine—deliberately choose to have children.

One in five American children born today is what was once called "illegitimate." In 1984, there were 770,000 births to unmarried women.[12] The birth rate for unmarried women is the highest ever recorded since the National Center for Health Statistics began keeping records in 1940. Americans are no longer shocked by out-of-wedlock births. Many baby boomers accept as natural—and even good—what was once a sin.

Sixty-five percent of out-of-wedlock births are to women aged 20 and older. Twenty-nine percent are to women aged 25 and older, and 11% are to women aged 30 and older. These aren't girls in trouble. They are women who choose to have children alone. Just as the baby boom inflates all birth statistics, it is behind the rise in births to unmarried women.

The number of births to unmarried women aged 30 and older rose 47% between 1980 and 1984, from 57,000 to 84,000.[13] As the peak of the baby boom fills the now-or-never age groups in the next decade, the number of births to unmarried older women will rise even more, reflecting the big decision that today's single women must make.

LIVING TOGETHER

The number of unmarried-couple households grew from 523,000 in 1970 to 2 million in 1986. Still, unmarried couples comprise only 2% of all American households.[14]

The people most likely to live together outside of marriage are young adults. As the baby boom filled the young adult age groups in the 1960s and 1970s, the number of unmarried couples grew faster than that of any other type of household. But fewer than 3% of baby boomers think that living together outside of marriage is the ideal lifestyle.[15] Most unmarried couples eventually marry or go their separate ways.

The growth in unmarried-couple households is slowing in the mid-1980s as the number of young adults declines because of the baby-bust generation. Living together outside of marriage is still a transitional stage in people's lives. It is likely to occur before marriage or between divorce and remarriage. In the next few decades, the number of unmarried couples should remain about what it is today, representing only a fraction of all American households.

GETTING MARRIED

More than nine out of ten baby-boom men and women believe marriage is the best lifestyle, and 83% say that love is the most important reason to marry.[16]

Baby boomers believe in marriage, though more than half their marriages will end in divorce. Today, 53% of baby-boom men and 59% of baby-boom women are married.[17] Ninety percent of baby boomers will have been married at least once in 20 years.

Just ten years ago, marriage was out of style. But how people feel about marriage has a lot to do with how old they are. When the baby boomers were teenagers and young adults intent on seeing the world, marriage was the last thing on their minds. A 1976 survey by the American Council on Life Insurance asked people aged 14 to 25 (those born from 1951 to 1962) what they thought about marriage. Only 32% said it was a ''great thing.'' Eighteen percent said people should seriously consider remaining unmarried.[18]

But the baby boomers changed their minds as they got older. The annual number of marriages in the United States has topped 2 million for more than a decade as the baby boom aged into its 20s.[19] The median age at which people marry for the first time is 25 for men and 23 for women.[20]

DIVORCE

But most of these marriages won't last. More than half of all baby-boom marriages will end in divorce.

As soon as the baby-boom generation came of age, the divorce statistics went through the roof. The number of divorces rose from about 400,000 a year in 1962 to 1.2 million in 1981. In 1982 and 1983, divorces dropped as the economic recession forced people to stay together—it takes money to divorce and set up two households where one was once enough.[21] Yet by 1985, with the economy improving, divorces were up again.[22]

The median age at which people divorce has remained relatively stable for the past decade—34 for men and 30 for women. Strangely enough, the seven-year itch is real. The median number of years that people are married before a divorce is seven.[23]

According to Census Bureau demographers Arthur Norton and Jeanne E. Moorman, nearly six out of ten baby boomers born between 1946 and 1955 who marry will eventually divorce. In contrast, only 28% of their parents will divorce. Among baby boomers born after 1955, about 50% will eventually divorce, Norton and Moorman project. The older baby boomers are most likely to divorce, say the researchers, because they ''represent the vanguard of the post-World War II baby boom. They were the first to encounter the obstacles confronting members of that disproportionately large population group.''[24] These obstacles include the war in Vietnam, the changes in women's roles, and the crowding of the job market, all of which can contribute to divorce.

Only about half of today's marriages are first marriages for both the bride and the groom.[25] In 1970, two out of three marriages were first marriages. Fully 22% of marriages today are a remarriage for either the bride or the groom, and 23% are a remarriage for both. The median age of a bride in a first marriage is 23; in a remarriage it is 33. For grooms, the median age in a first marriage is 25; in a remarriage it is 36. These are the strands that make up the web of complexity in the baby boom's families.

Couples are more likely to divorce today because the traditional ties that bind men and women have weakened, according to Johns Hopkins family specialist Andrew J. Cherlin. ''The greater economic independence of women means that marriage is less necessary as an economic partnership,'' says Cherlin.[26] Consequently, couples judge their marriage by how well it meets their emotional needs. If it doesn't stack up, they divorce.

Or, as author Bryant Robey puts it, "Divorce is not a rejection of marriage, it's just a personal rejection."[27] When it's love that holds marriages together, not money or children, the emotional whims of husband and wife can crack the foundation of the relationship.

As the two-earner family becomes more firmly lodged in American life, and as the economy adjusts to this new norm, however, the economic partnership of husband and wife will regain its importance. This could mean that divorce rates will fall; then again, while it might take two to tango, no one has to dance with the same partner all the time.

Because of divorce, it's getting harder for couples to reach their silver wedding anniversary. Though most couples (63%) will celebrate 10 years together, less than half (41%) will celebrate 25 years of marriage. Only 25% will stay together for 40 years, and just 13% will make it to their golden anniversary—50 years of marriage—as divorce and death take their toll.[28]

A baby boomer marriage will last an average of 23 years, while their parents' marriages will last 32 years, on average. The baby boom's higher propensity for divorce makes its marriages shorter than those of its parents.

But the longer husband and wife stay together, the less likely they are to ever divorce, because divorce usually occurs in the first years of a marriage. Couples who make it to their ninth wedding anniversary, for example, can expect to be together for another 25 years. Those who celebrate 15 years together can expect to enjoy another 23.

One unusual explanation for the rise in divorce is that people are living longer. Death once gave people a way out of a bad relationship; now divorce is the only way out. If couples do not divorce, they can expect to spend 44 years together, including 13 years after the children are grown up and gone. At the turn of the century, couples could expect to spend only 34 years together, with just a year or two in the empty nest before the death of a spouse.[29] Untimely death is not as likely to end an unhappy relationship today.

Since the median age at marriage is 23 for women and 25 for men, and since people stay married for a median of seven years before they divorce, the people most likely to divorce are those in their early 30s. The number of adults in the divorce-prone age group, 25 to 39, will not peak until 1990, according to demographer Paul C. Glick.[30] This means that the number of divorces should remain high until the middle of the 1990s. Glick projects that the number of first marriages will start to drop before the end of the 1980s, while divorces and remarriages will rise slightly. But second divorces are becoming more common.

Looking back on their lives, this is what the baby boomers will see: 90% will have married once; half will have divorced once. One in three will have married twice, and one in five will have divorced twice. Five percent of baby boomers will have divorced three times.[31]

HAVING CHILDREN

When Peter Townshend, formerly of The Who, drives through London with his family past the apartment in which he wrote "My Generation," his children complain that he's shown them that apartment too many times before. They know the story of the generation that grew up on rock and roll. They're not interested; they have their own passions.[32]

Like every generation before it, the baby boom is passing the torch to a younger generation. But the boomers have been slow to do this, relishing their youth. Middle age takes a bigger bite of the baby boom every year, and old age now looms on the not-so-distant horizon. The commitment to having children may be the generation's final nod to the fact that no one lives forever.

The baby boom waited longer to have children—and is having fewer children—than any other generation in American history. Demographers predict that nearly 20% of baby-boom women will never have children.[33] Among women born from 1951 to 1955, 18% will never have children, says economist David E. Bloom of Harvard University. Among those born from 1956 to 1960, 16% will be childless. The generation's propensity to divorce is one reason that it is less likely to have children.

Another reason is the changing American economy. Neither baby-boom women nor baby-boom men can afford to have as many children as they want. So they delay and limit, falling short of their ideals. Only 1% of men and women believe the ideal family is childless.[34] Yet as many as one in five baby boomers will have no children. Only 3% of men and women believe the ideal family has just one child—yet another 25% of baby boomers will stop at one.

Over half of men and women say the two-child family is ideal, but many will fall short of that goal. Those who reach it will do so only by sacrificing money and time. The young adults of the 1950s did not have to make these sacrifices because men's and women's roles were neatly divided. The parents of the baby boom had the money and the time to raise a family.

THE CHILDLESS

Half of women in their 20s and one-fifth of women in their 30s have not yet had children, according to the Census Bureau. The proportion of women who are still childless at ages 25 to 29 and 30 to 34 is more than double what it was during the 1950s.[35]

Baby-boom women are having fewer children than their mothers did for complex but compelling sociological and economic reasons. As mentioned earlier, baby-boom women are more educated than their mothers, and educated women are more likely to work. Working women have smaller families, on average, than housewives. Women are more likely to work today because there are more opportunities for them than there were in the 1950s, and because their families depend on their incomes.

"In a world where it is becoming the norm for women to work, the economic impact of children is particularly hard on mothers," says Harvard's David E. Bloom.[36] "As skill requirements for jobs increase, it is more costly for women to have children, especially before they establish a career."

University of Maryland economist Frank Levy agrees. "Before 1973, when real wages were growing, a single earner could afford to spend more even when his family grew in size. But since 1973, young families have tried to keep consumption growing in the face of stagnant wages."[37] One of the ways they have done this is by delaying childbearing. "Since 1973," says Levy, "the average number of children per married couple has fallen from 1.2 to 0.97—a 20 percent drop in the number of young mouths that need feeding."

White, highly educated, pursuing a career—these characteristics describe the woman who puts off having children today. Education is by far the most important variable that affects the timing of childbearing. As American women gain in education, they wait longer to have children.

The Census Bureau reports that among women aged 25 to 34 with a postgraduate degree, 63% were childless in 1985.[38] Among those with a college degree, 59% are childless. In contrast, only 34% of all women aged 25 to 34 have no children.

Among women aged 35 to 44, 30% of those with a graduate degree and 26% of those with a college degree are childless, compared to 14% of all women in that age group.

There are four types of childless baby boomers: those who can't have children because they are infertile; those who could have children but don't want them; those who are forced by circumstances beyond their control (such as divorce) to remain childless; and those who are delaying having children.[39]

"Many childless women may not formally choose to remain childless," say researchers Anne R. Pebley and

David E. Bloom, "but do so only because they have postponed having a child until it is too late."[40]

The typical childless woman, according to Pebley and Bloom, is well educated, working, not devoutly religious, and more likely than other women to be divorced. High-income couples are also more likely to be childless. "These are the characteristics of a group whose members are likely to be economically successful and to have many options in life," say Pebley and Bloom.[41]

Childless couples live differently than couples with children. They have more money to spend on luxuries. They are more likely to buy theater tickets, video and stereo equipment, a sports car, expensive clothes, vacations, and gourmet food. The childless travel more, hire more household help, and eat out more. Childless women, because they can devote their undivided attention to their work, are likely to advance further in their careers than women with children.

The rise in childlessness will change the way in which we care for the elderly, suggest Pebley and Bloom. The childless elderly will have to rely on their friends for care and companionship. But their friends also will be old, and as the health of the childless fails with age, they may wish that they had invested in a younger generation to help them out.

The childless baby boomers can spend a lifetime swapping stories with one another about the horrors of pregnancy, infants, and teenagers. Most will be glad they don't have children because parents complain about the sleepless nights, the cost of shoes, the crowded bathrooms, the lack of time for themselves. But every now and then the childless may wonder whether they missed something significant.

The world the baby boom created is a cafeteria of choices. As the baby boom passes the displays of opportunities, it loads its tray with a rewarding career, a middle-class lifestyle, and children. But at the cash register, it can't afford to have them all. In an ideal world, the baby boom would have more children. In the real world, many baby boomers are leaving children on the shelf.

INFERTILITY

Only 14% of married couples of childbearing age are infertile, a proportion that has remained stable for decades.[42] But the ranks of the infertile are growing because millions of baby boomers are in the childbearing ages, and they are getting older. The older the couple, the more likely that husband or wife will be infertile. Solving the fertility problems of the baby boom is a big business today in part because the generation has waited so long to have children.

Couples are classified as infertile when they have not used birth control for one year but have not become pregnant. Among wives aged 20 to 24, only 11% are infertile. But among wives aged 40 to 44, 27% are infertile. As baby boom couples delay having children, some discover that they have delayed too long and can't have children at all.

This is one reason why demographers predict that so many baby-boom women will never have children. But only 10% say they don't want children, according to the Census Bureau.[43] Couples who want children but can't have them are creating a new industry that includes artificial insemination, in vitro fertilization, surrogate mothers, and other new reproductive technologies. The ethics of the new technologies will be hotly debated through the 1990s, but the ethical questions won't stop the scientific advances, because there are too many child-less couples demanding to have children.

In the back of many of the nation's newspapers can be found more evidence of the baby boom's longing for children: advertisements from childless couples who want to adopt. Strangely enough, the number of babies available for adoption fell in the past decade, just when demand surged.

Americans adopted only 142,000 children in 1982, the latest statistics available, but most of these children were adopted by relatives.[44] Since 1972, the number of children adopted by nonrelatives fell by 22% because only 7% of unwed mothers put their children up for adoption, a smaller proportion than in the past. Most unwed mothers keep their babies.

One way baby boomers cope with the shortage of babies is by adopting children from other countries. In 1984, Americans adopted 8000 foreign children, most of them from Korea. But this number meets only a fraction of the demand.

PREVENTING BIRTHS

An astounding 47% of baby-boom couples are ster-ile.[45] But most of them chose to become sterile because they had had all the children they wanted. Among married women aged 30 to 34, 44% are surgically sterile (or their husbands are sterile); among women aged 35 to 39, 58% are sterile, as are 67% of those aged 40 to 44.

Sterilization ends childbearing forever. Many baby boomers who are not ready for such a permanent solution depend on a variety of birth control devices to delay or space children. The use of birth control means that baby-boom women are less likely to have children they don't want than were their mothers. Today, 30% of babies are unwanted or came along at the wrong time, down from 66% in 1965.[46]

But there are still many unwanted pregnancies: More than 1 million women have abortions each year in the United States.[47] The success with which women prevent unwanted births depends on the type of birth control they use. Among married women using the pill, only 2 in 100 get pregnant in a year. But one woman in ten who relies on condoms finds herself pregnant within a year, along with 14% of those who use a diaphragm. For those relying on the rhythm method, nearly one in five becomes pregnant each year.[48]

There are many more pregnancies than births each year in the United States. In 1981, for example, there were nearly 6 million pregnancies; only 60% resulted in a birth.[49] Thirteen percent ended in a miscarriage and 26% in an abortion. If women did not have the abortion option, 5 million babies would be born each year in the United States instead of fewer than 4 million. While companies that sell baby products might welcome these births, they would hurt the American economy. Women—who make up 44% of all workers—would have to raise more children than our economy provides time or money for.

THE BABY BOOM'S CHILDREN

The baby boomers vowed to change the way society worked. They wanted to do this by raising children differently, freeing them from stereotyped roles, but they discovered that this is not a simple task.

In a study of how successful young adults were in raising children differently, two professors at the University of California at Los Angeles tracked parents aged 18 to 35 beginning in 1974. Their study included both conventional and unconventional families (unmarried couples, single parents, and people in communes) to determine whether unconventional families would raise their children differently from conventional ones.

The unconventional parents said they wanted to rear their children in a natural environment, allowing them to be emotionally expressive. They did not want them using plastic products or commercially manufactured toys. They prepared their own baby food and breast fed for a lengthy period. The researchers found, however, that these parents' ideals were tempered in actual practice. "What might have become extensive, even extreme innovations, judging from the parents' goals and plans at the time their child was born, were limited in actual practice," the researchers reported in *Psychology Today*.[50]

In fact, the differences in the childrearing practices of the two groups were small in comparison to childrearing practices in other countries of the world. In the end, the changes in childrearing made by the unconventional families proved to be only an American variation, not a new approach.

Though the goals of the unconventional families were only modestly met, these families succeeded in emphasizing to their children equality between men and women, concern for the environment, and the importance of the community of friends and family. "They may have provided their children with the skill to adapt to different circumstances with more than one model and script for conduct," the researchers concluded.[51]

No other goal is of greater importance to parents than that their children be happy. The jury is still out on whether the baby boom's children will be happy and well-adjusted adults, or whether they will be seriously troubled because of their parents' lifestyles.

The baby boom's life has been one of extraordinary change. The children of the baby boom may have smoother sailing. They may see the change in their parents' lives and come to expect change in their own lives. Change is a constant, and people who are open to change are happier than those troubled by each shift in course. The baby boom may be raising children who can adapt. The daughters of the baby boomers will have more role models on which to shape their lives. The sons will know that the breadwinner burden is not theirs alone to shoulder. Diversity is what the baby boom's children learn every day by example.

In fact, the baby boom's ever-changing lifestyle may be a healthier way to raise children than the nuclear-family isolation of the 1950s. A depressed, resentful mother imprisoned in the house can damage the psychological well-being of her children; the lack of intellectual fulfillment exacts its toll. On the other hand, divorce, remarriage, stepparents, working parents, day care, and a latchkey lifestyle take their toll as well. The baby boom will find out how much of a toll, and its children are the guinea pigs.

CHILDREN AND DIVORCE

Every year, the parents of over 1 million children divorce. Fifty-nine percent of the baby boom's children will live with only one parent for at least a year before reaching the age of 18, according to Census Bureau demographer Arthur J. Norton.[52] Thirty-five percent will live with a stepparent during part of their childhood.

Despite the rise in births since the mid-1970s, the number of married couples with children had been declining as divorce broke up families. Between 1970 and 1985, the number of married couples with children fell by 5%. During these same years, the number of single-parent families doubled.[53] Between 1985 and 1986, the number of married couples with children edged up for the first time in many years, but the number of single-parent families also continued to rise.

Seven million Americans are raising children alone. Most of these solitary parents (nine out of ten) are women. Families headed by women have made up a significant share of American households for decades. But women today are heading families for different reasons than women in the past. In 1940, a woman heading a family alone was likely to be a middle-aged widow with older children.[54] Today, women heading families are likely to be separated or divorced, and half have children younger than age 6. Most are struggling to make ends meet.

The median income of single-parent families headed by women is just one-third of the median income of married couples with children. Upon divorce, a woman's income drops to 70% of its predivorce level, according to

University of Michigan researchers Greg J. Duncan and Saul D. Hoffman.[55] But most single parents remarry within five years. Upon remarriage, a woman's income is 27% greater than what it was before her divorce and about the same as it would have been if she had stayed with her first husband.

Remarriages are complicated by children. Forty percent of the remarriages of baby boomers include a child from a previous marriage, say researchers Arland Thornton and Deborah Freedman, making the new marriage unstable—remarriages that involve stepchildren are more likely to end in divorce than those that don't.[56] Fully 17% of marriages that are remarriages for both husband and wife and that involve stepchildren break up within three years, according to researchers Lynn K. White and Alan Booth of the University of Nebraska.[57]

Because of stepparents and stepchildren, families today include complex parent–child relationships. In 1981, only two-thirds of American children lived with both biological parents, according to the National Health Interview Survey.[58] Less than half of all children will live out their childhood in this kind of family.

Stepfamilies are changing the definition of "immediate family." A divorced mother would include her children in her immediate family, but she would probably not include her ex-husband, says family specialist Andrew Cherlin. But if the children still see their father regularly, they might include both their father and their mother in their immediate family. "One can no longer define 'the family' or 'the immediate family' except in relation to a particular person," Cherlin concludes.[59]

Most children whose parents separate live with their mother, and they don't see much of their father. Over half see their father less than once a month, including 31% who never see their father, report Suzanne M. Bianchi of the Census Bureau and Judith A. Seltzer of the University of Wisconsin. Only one-quarter of the children of divorced parents see their father at least once a week.[60]

Children who live with their mother and a stepfather see their father even less frequently. Forty-six percent never see him. Only 8% see him at least once a week.

No one knows what effect divorce and remarriage will have on the children of the baby boom. A few decades ago, children of divorced parents were an oddity. Today they are the majority. The fact that divorce is the norm may make it easier for children to accept their parents' divorce. But what will it do to their marriages in the decades ahead? No one will know until it's too late to do anything about it.

CHILDBEARING

At the peak of the baby boom in 1957, 36 million women of childbearing age gave birth to more than 4.3 million babies.[61] In 1985, over 50 million women of childbearing age had only 3.7 million babies because American fertility is half of what it was in 1957.[62]

The fertility rate (the number of babies born in a year for every 1000 women aged 15 to 44) fell to an historic low in the mid-1970s—only 65 babies were born each year for every 1000 women of childbearing age. The fertility rate today remains at 65, down from its peak in 1957, when 120 babies were born for every 1000 women of childbearing age.

For two centuries, American families have been shrinking. In 1800, the average woman had seven children. By the 1930s, the average was two. Then the mothers of the baby boom upset history, having three and four children apiece. The baby-boom women, who are averaging only 1.8 children each, are following the small-family traditions of their grandmothers.

Births have been rising in the past few years—from a low of 3.1 million in 1973 to 3.7 million in 1985—because there are so many women of childbearing age. It's not another baby boom as much as it is a parent boom. Because the baby boom is in the childbearing ages, it is inflating the number of parents and potential parents in the population. Births should peak at about 3.8 million in 1988 before beginning a gradual decline as the baby-boom generation moves out of the childbearing ages.

THE NEW FATHER

For couples lucky enough to stay together, both mother and father are caring for the kids. The new role of the father has blurred traditional sex roles in the home; it's a radical change from the 1950s, when women changed diapers and men went to work. Today's fathers are taking childbirth classes, coaching in the delivery room, and changing diapers. Ninety percent of expectant mothers say their husbands will help them care for their babies, according to a Gallup/Levi's poll of new mothers.[63] Eighty-five percent say their husbands will change the baby's diapers. (The poll did not ask expectant fathers how they felt about this!)

Mothers today breastfeed their babies. This is another important difference between baby-boom women and their mothers, who were discouraged from breastfeeding by doctors in the 1950s. Today, 53% of new mothers breastfeed their babies. The more educated the mother, the more likely she is to breastfeed. Among new mothers with at least one year of college, 73% breastfeed their babies.[64]

Despite the fact that baby-boom couples are more likely to plan their babies than their parents were, they still are not having their babies when they want them. When fertility researchers ask women which month is the best for giving birth, the answer is April. Yet except for February (the short month), fewer babies are born in April than in any other month of the year. When researchers ask women which is the worst month to have a baby, most say August. Yet that is the month when births peak.

What creates this paradox? According to researchers Joseph Lee Rodgers and J. Richard Udry, many couples who want an April birth stop using birth control in July, thinking that they will become pregnant right away.[65] But pregnancy typically occurs three or four months after a couple stops using birth control. Instead of being born in April as planned, the baby is born in August.

Births once occurred randomly by day of the week. A baby was just as likely to be born on a Sunday as on a Wednesday. That was before childbirth went high-tech and doctors scheduled more convenient delivery days. Now that doctors deliver one out of five babies by cesarean section, they can arrange deliveries around a 9-to-5 schedule and take their weekends off.

Monday through Friday, there are an average of more than 10,000 births a day in the United States. Saturdays and Sundays have the fewest births, fewer than 9000 on average, according to the National Center for Health Statistics.[66]

Fully 99% of American babies are born in hospitals. Doctors deliver almost all of them, but the baby boom's preference for natural childbirth shows up in the statistics. Midwives are delivering an increasing number of babies. In 1984, they delivered 78,000, 51% more than in 1980, according to the National Center for Health Statistics. Still, midwives assist at only a fraction of all births.

THE FIRST BIRTH

Most baby-boom women already have children. Twenty-one percent have one child; 24% have two, and 17% have three or more.[67]

The childless are the majority among baby-boom women in their early 20s. But 60% of women in their late 20s have at least one child. Among women in their early 30s, 75% have children, and among those in their late 30s, 85% are mothers. Though most baby boomers have small families, one-third of baby-boom women in their late 30s have at least three children.

Most women have children when they are in their 20s. But a large proportion of baby-boom women are waiting until their 30s to have their first child. Though the number of women having their first baby at age 30 or older is relatively small—only 197,000 in 1984 (among 1.5 million first births in that year)—the proportion of all first births accounted for by older mothers is significant.[68]

In 1970, only 4% of first births were to women aged 30 and older. Today, 13% of first births are to older mothers—who are likely to be educated professionals with high family incomes. Forty-five percent of new mothers aged 30 and older are college graduates, compared with only 12% of new mothers younger than age 30.

In a study of mature first-time mothers, Judith Langer, president of Langer Associates, Inc., a consumer research firm in New York, asked them why they finally decided to have a baby. Most of the mothers said they felt the pressure of the biological clock—it was now or never, and they chose now. Because of their age, most of the women thought they were better prepared for parenthood than younger women. The older women had years of freedom that the younger mothers did not.

But there are drawbacks, according to Langer's study. Older mothers have difficulty finding the energy and patience to care for young children, and many are unhappy that they cannot have as many children as they want because of their age.

"Men's changing roles came through dramatically in this study," Langer says. "The new involved father is a reality—yet for most couples this does not mean a 50–50 division of duties. While the women repeatedly said that their husbands participated in parenthood by preparing for childbirth and by sharing child care and household responsibilities, most of the women assumed that, whether or not they had jobs, they still had the primary parenting responsibility."[69]

Do men drop the ball, or do women refuse to pass it to them? Despite all the talk about men's and women's roles and what men and women should do, when it comes to taking care of children, many women want to be in charge. According to studies by Wellesley College professor Joseph H. Pleck, new mothers dominate new fathers in relating to their infants. Many new fathers withdraw, and women end up with most of the parenting responsibility. It's not enough for men to be willing to take on a greater role in childrearing—women must be willing to let them.[70]

The first birth separates people into two camps—those who have children and those who don't. When people have their first child, it's a turning point in their lives. Today, a large share of babies are first-borns because people have fewer children. If couples have only two children, on average, then half of all births will be the first birth and half will be the second child. Because most families today have two or three children, 42% of births are first births. In the 1950s, just 25% of babies were first-borns.[71]

People spend more money on their first baby than on their second or third. New parents must buy all the baby paraphernalia for the first one, but they can reuse equipment and clothes when they have their second or third. Parents spend only 69% as much on a second child as on a first, according to estimates by Lawrence Olson, vice president of SAGE Associates, Inc., a Washington, D.C. consulting firm.[72]

Before their first child's first birthday, new parents can expect to spend between $3000 and $5500, according to estimates by *The Wall Street Journal*, not including the $3200 average cost of a hospital delivery. These costs include a car seat, a crib, a highchair, a stroller, a changing table, a diaper pail, food and clothing. A year's worth of disposable diapers costs over $500.[73]

The nesting instinct boosts buying in other ways as well. At the time of a first birth, new parents are more likely to buy houses, cars, and appliances, and they are even more likely to go on vacation than other people, according to the market research firm Leo J. Shapiro & Associates of Chicago.[74]

The companies that sell children's products and services are doing brisk business now. They are likely to continue to boom through the 1990s as the baby boom feathers its nests. Because most baby boomers won't have many children, they can spend more on the few they have. Grandparents, too, will provide a bounty of toys and good times for their few grandchildren. During the next couple of decades, many baby boomers will have to shelter their children not from hardship, but from too many good intentions.

THE ONLY CHILD

Only 3% of women believe one child is ideal, but at least one in ten—and perhaps as many as one in four—will have just one child.[75] The concept of having only one never has been popular among parents for many reasons: parents want playmates for their children, they want their children to have brothers and sisters, they want a son and a daughter, and they worry that only children are selfish and unhappy.

Studies show, however, that only children have advantages in life that children with brothers and sisters do not. Researchers at the University of Texas analyzed the well-being of adults who are only children and found them to be as happy as or happier than people with brothers and sisters. Adults who are only children report that their lives are exciting, that their health is excellent, that their family life is good, and that they get a great deal of satisfaction out of their friendships. On all of these measures, only children rate equal to or higher than adults who have brothers and sisters. Men who are only children are more likely to be "very happy" than men who have siblings; for women, the proportion who are "very happy" is about the same whether a woman is an only child or not.

Only children develop greater self-esteem and self-sufficiency as adults, suggest the researchers, because their parents are economically better off due to their small family size, and because only children receive their parents' undivided attention. "If reluctance to have an only child is based primarily on fear that he or she will be unusually likely to become a maladjusted and unhappy adult," the researchers conclude, "we believe that the best available evidence indicates that the reluctance is ill-founded."[76]

Despite these findings, most baby boomers will have a second child before their first child is five years old.

SENDING CHILDREN TO SCHOOL

It's no coincidence that just as the baby boom's children enter elementary school, parents across the country demand better teachers, better textbooks, and a better curriculum. The best-educated generation in American history will pressure the public schools to upgrade through the 1990s.

Now that the baby boom's toddlers are in nursery school, America's private school enrollment is growing once again. In 1965, only 11% of 3- and 4-year-olds were enrolled in school. Today, nearly 40% are, according to the Census Bureau, and most nursery-school students attend private school.[77] Baby-boom parents are already paying for day care and nursery school. It may not be a big step for them to pay for elementary and secondary schooling in the 1990s and 2000s. This is what worries the public school administrators who foresee a growing split between private and public school students.

Today, private schools enroll 5 million students— from nursery school through high school—accounting for 14% of all students. While total school enrollment has fallen in the past decade because the baby-bust generation is in the elementary and secondary grades, private-school enrollment has increased, pushed up by the baby-boom children as they swell attendance in private nursery school and kindergarten classrooms. Private elementary- and secondary-school enrollments, which have been stable for the past decade, may rise as the baby boom's children enter first grade, especially if the public schools can't satisfy the baby boom that its children are getting a good education.

In 1965, 15% of elementary-school students and 11% of high-school students attended private schools. Today, only 11% of elementary-school and 9% of high-school students are in private school. Most private-school students go to Catholic schools, but Catholic-school enrollments have been shrinking while non-Catholic private-school enrollment has grown.[78] If the baby boom decides to send its children to private schools in the years ahead, nondenominational schools may become even more popular, since only 30% of baby boomers are Catholic. For teachers unhappy with the public-school system, the next two decades will offer them an opportunity to open private schools that will satisfy the baby boom's demand for quality education.

The higher a family's income, the more likely it is to send its children to private school. Among school-age children from households in the highest income category ($50,000 and over), more than 25% go to private school. Among those in the lowest income category, only 3% go to private school. The more educated the parents, the more likely their children are to go to private school. Among children whose parents have gone to graduate school, one-fifth go to private school. Among those whose parents stopped with a high-school diploma, only 9% attend private school.

These statistics bode well for private schools in the 1990s, as well-educated, affluent baby-boom couples see their children off to school. Just as marriage will polarize the lifestyles of the baby boom in the years ahead, it could polarize their children as well. The public schools could become, increasingly, the place where children from single-parent families learn.

ARRANGED ALMA MATERS

Since more than half of baby boomers have been to college for at least one year, most baby boomers will want their children to go to college. In fact, 86% of families with children expect their kids to go to college, according to Market Facts, a Chicago-based market research firm.[79] But only 54% of these families are saving money for college expenses. Among families headed by baby boomers, fewer than half are saving for their children's college education.

U.S. News and World Report estimates that tuition, fees, and room and board at the typical private university could cost $30,000 a year by the turn of the century.[80] Public universities, though less expensive, won't be bargains either. The University of Michigan expects four years of tuition to cost $25,000 by the turn of the century.

The costs of private colleges increased 179% between 1974 and 1986, faster than the 118% increase in the cost of living and the rise in wages.[81] College costs are now so great that many baby boomers have little hope of paying for their children's college education. But financial institutions and the colleges themselves are trying to salvage the baby boom's hope, experimenting with unique ways of helping them.

Zero coupon bonds, for example, are an increasingly popular way to finance college costs. Parents can buy a bond for only a few thousand dollars when their child is young. The bond matures, and by the time the child is ready for college it is worth much more than the parents paid for it—perhaps enough to cover the cost of a year's tuition. If parents buy a zero coupon bond each year for four consecutive years, then they will have paid for their child's college tuition years before the bills are due.

Parents can also pay tuition costs directly, long before their child is old enough to go to college. By paying a lump sum to Duquesne University, for example, parents can buy four years of tuition. The younger the child, the lower the lump-sum payment. For a newborn, parents pay only about $5000 now. Duquesne guarantees them four years of tuition in 18 years. But if a child does not qualify for admission to Duquesne, the parents get back only their initial investment; they lose the accrued interest. The other catch: their child must spend at least one year at Duquesne before he or she can transfer to another school (after that, Duquesne will pay its own tuition costs to the other school).

There's a tremendous business opportunity in bridging the gap between the baby boom's desires for its children and its ability to pay. Already, brokers are stepping in to handle the details. The creators of the Duquesne plan expect to have 120 schools signed up in the early tuition plan by the end of 1987. In a few years, baby boomers may be able to pick and choose from hundreds of schools, including their own alma maters.

The prepayment plans will allow many of the baby boom's children to go to college who otherwise could not. But the plans may change the process of leaving home. No longer will high-school students pore over college catalogs, mail off applications, and wait for an answer. They will know from grade school on which school they must attend.

The plans will thus become a perfect target for a new generation of rebels. Imagine the uproar when the ungrateful teenager announces he would rather drop dead than go to the college for which his parents have already paid.

THE BABY BOOM AT HOME

More than two decades ago, Betty Friedan labeled the home a "comfortable concentration camp" that imprisoned women in "endless, monotonous, unrewarding" work.[82] Not long after *The Feminine Mystique* made the bestseller list, the walls of the camp tumbled down. Millions of women went to work, and the teenage baby-boom generation left home to explore politics, college, and new ways of life. Today, only 20% of American women are housewives. In 1960, one out of two women was a housewife.

The lives of Americans changed dramatically since 1960, and the home is the stage on which these changes took place. Women and men transformed the concentration camp into a campground. No longer prisoners in the home, women became campers who never fully settled in because they were too busy with outside interests. "Pup tenting" is what market researcher Judith Langer calls this lifestyle.

Yet today the home is rising in importance in American life. For the next two decades, it will rival the position it held in the 1950s as the middle-aged dominate the nation's attention. In the 1990s and 2000s, most baby boomers will marry, most will have children, and most will own homes.

The suburban ranch, the house on the corner, the renovated saltbox—these are the homes the baby boom is learning to love. The single-family, detached home is by far the house of choice for the generation, as it is for every generation. A study by *Professional Builder* finds that 85% of homebuyers want a detached, single-family house.[83] The firm Analysis and Forecasting, Inc., projects that over 90% of baby-boom homeowners will live in a single-family house by the turn of the century.[84] Only 6% will live in co-ops or condominiums, while 4% will live in mobile homes.

And the baby boomers don't want just any house— they want houses with room enough to raise a couple of kids, according to William C. Apgar, Jr., of MIT. Though the average size of new homes declined from 1667 to 1536 square feet in the early 1980s as housing prices skyrocketed, the average size of new homes is on its way up again—to 1540 square feet in 1985.[85]

The baby boom accounted for over 80% of first-time homebuyers and half of repeat buyers in 1985.[86] First-time homebuyers are looking for starter homes— something big enough for two people, possibly three. Repeat homebuyers want bigger homes, large enough to put some space between themselves and their teenagers. First-time homebuyers bought a median 1292 square feet of home in 1985; repeat buyers bought homes that averaged 1620 squre feet. First-time buyers paid a median of $65,000 for their homes; repeat buyers paid $84,500.

Home ownership will flourish in the 1990s as repeat buyers dominate the housing market, predict Rutgers University housing experts George Sternlieb and James W. Hughes. "Baby-boom couples will be more fertile with income than with offspring, edging the housing market upscale," they say.[87] Those who bought condominiums or small single-family homes when that was all they could afford will buy bigger and better homes as their incomes rise.

But the rental market will suffer. Renters are most likely to be young people, and the number of young adults in the American population will shrink for the next 15 years as the baby-bust generation enters its 20s. Baby boomers who invested in rental property may want to reexamine its potential for growth. In a college town, the potential will remain. Elsewhere, rental property may lose value.

THE DISAPPEARANCE OF THE HOUSEWIFE

Two-thirds of baby boomers want an egalitarian marriage in which husband and wife share the tasks of earning money, housekeeping, and child care, according to the Virginia Slims American Women's Poll.[88]

The disappearance of the institution of the housewife has been so rapid and profound that many American businesses, churches, and volunteer organizations have been caught between statistics and instincts. Most Americans were raised by full-time housewives. This is what makes the image of the housewife so powerful, though she is nearly extinct. Fewer than 11% of women today are the stereotypical housewife—married, not working, raising children. Among housewives, women aged 65 and older are the single largest group.[89]

The number of housewives has fallen by at least 30% in every age group younger than age 55 since 1970, while the number aged 55 to 64 crept up by 4% and those aged 65 and older grew by 21%. Because housewives are aging, most have no children at home; only 24% of housewives today take care of preschoolers.

When widows and women who head single-parent families are included in the count of full-time homemakers, the number rises to 31 million (this number does not include elderly women who are retired from the labor force), down only 5% since 1970 because of the rapid growth in the number of elderly widows. One-third of full-time homemakers are women aged 65 or older, and more than half are aged 55 or older.

Like the ranks of railroad conductors, the number of homemakers will shrink further in the years ahead as working women of the baby-boom generation replace older housewives. By 1995, only about one in seven women younger than age 45 will be a full-time homemaker.

Thirty-three percent of women who work would rather be housewives, but this proportion is not much greater than the 21% of working men who say they would rather stay at home, according to a 1983 *New York Times* poll.[90] Nearly half of working women—47% in 1985—regard their work as a career, according to the Roper poll, up from 30% in 1971.[91] Women today are almost as career-oriented as men, 57% of whom regard their work as a career.

Even the baby-boom women who are full-time homemakers view homemaking as a stage in their lives, not their lifetime career. Overall, one-third of full-time homemakers plan to work, but among those aged 18 to 29, fully 64% plan to work, and among those aged 30 to 44, over half want to work, according to the poll.[92] Increasingly, even full-time homemakers regard housekeeping as a part-time job. This means that they expect husbands and children to help out more.

MEN AND HOUSEWORK

Most women—whether they work outside the home or not—expect men to take on some housekeeping chores. Eighty-three percent of employed women and 72% of homemakers, for example, agree that "men should be as responsible for home cleaning as women are," according to a 1983 Good Housekeeping Institute report.[93]

Though wives still do more housework than husbands, baby-boom men do more than their fathers. Sixty-three percent of wives aged 18 to 29 and 58% of those aged 30 to 39 say that their husbands do some, half, or most of the household chores.[94]

Overall, men aged 25 to 44 did 14 hours of housework a week, according to a 1981 study, up from 11 hours in 1975.[95] Women aged 25 to 44 spent 33 hours a week on housework in 1975, and 32 hours a week in 1981.

The housekeeping standards of the 1950s depended upon a full-time housewife who dusted, vacuumed, scrubbed, and cooked each day. Working women today can't and don't need to do as much housework as their mothers. When women go to work full time, they spend much less time doing housework. Consequently, the share of housework done by the husband rises dramatically if his wife works full time.

Married women who work full time spend only two hours each weekday on housework (not including child care), according to William Michelson in a 1980 time-use study of married couples in Toronto.[96] This is only half of the four hours of housework done each day by women who work part time, and less than half of the five hours of housework done each day by housewives.

The husbands of women with full-time jobs spent 57 minutes doing housework each weekday, Michelson found. This is only 9 minutes more than the 48 minutes of housework done daily by the husbands of women who work part time, and only 14 minutes more than the 43 minutes of housework done each day by the husbands of housewives.

But those 57 minutes of housekeeping done by the husbands of women who work full time account for fully one-third of the family's housework. The husbands of women who work part time do only 17% of the housework and those married to housewives do only 12%.

One-third of husbands today are married to women who work full time—17 million of the nation's 50 million married men. Among baby-boom husbands, fully 43% are married to women who work full time.[97]

A large percentage of today's husbands do as much cooking and cleaning as their wives. Among wives who work full time, 24% divide housekeeping chores evenly, according to the Virginia Slims Poll.[98]

In addition, the husbands of women who work full time are responsible for much of the child care. Michelson's study of Toronto families revealed that fathers spent 40 minutes a day in primary child care (meaning such tasks as diapering, feeding, and bathing) when their children were younger than age four. Mothers who worked full time spent between one and two hours a day in primary child care.

WOMEN AND HOUSEWORK

Though housewives do more housework than working women, both do less housework than they once did. More than two-thirds of women—including working women and homemakers—agree that "over the years, I have relaxed my housekeeping standards a great deal," according to a report by the Good Housekeeping Institute.[99] Sixty-one percent of homemakers and 50% of working women say they feel liberated from the worry over housecleaning.

Many businesses are hurting because housekeeping standards are lower than they used to be. Take the bedsheet industry, for example. The number of bedsheets sold in the United States—at 30 million dozen—is no greater today than it was 20 years ago, depite the fact that there are 58 million more Americans sleeping on sheets, according to Peter Francese, President of American Demographics.[100] People aren't changing their sheets as often as they once did. The full-time housewife changed the sheets on her family's beds once a week. When the sheets looked threadbare, she bought new ones. Many of today's new homemakers are lucky if they change their sheets once a month. They're too busy to notice whether the sheets are worn, and even if they notice, they probably don't care, says Francese.

Because dual-earner couples do less housework than traditional couples, they spend less on housekeeping products and more on household help. The Bureau of Labor Statistics' Consumer Expenditure Surveys show that dual-earner couples spend proportionately less on housekeeping supplies than traditional couples, but more on domestic services, such as maids and babysitters.

A few decades ago, businesses appealed to the homemaker by telling her that she was a professional involved in complex housekeeping tasks. Today, the marketing of household products has taken a 180-degree turn as men and women—whether they are working or not—have little time for housecleaning.

On the list of activities that people do every day, housecleaning ranks lowest in satisfaction, according to a University of Michigan study.[101] Until a few years ago, marketers sold household products by pretending that housecleaning was fun. Today, a woman is "more likely to buy a VCR than a vacuum cleaner," says market researcher Judith Langer.[102] The way to market housecleaning products now is to sell convenience.

Eighty-seven percent of housewives and 89% of working women report that they "prefer to buy a few cleaning products that can be used for a variety of cleaning tasks rather than buy a number of specialty cleaners designed for specific cleaning needs," according to the Good Housekeeping Institute study.[103] Seventy-three percent of full-time homemakers and 79% of employed women "look for anything that is quicker or easier to use."[104] And among product claims, over 90% of working women and homemakers are most interested in buying products that are convenient and save time.

Baby-boom women don't have the time to be the housekeepers their mothers were. Baby-boom men have few excuses for not pitching in. The lives of baby-boom men and women have merged in the work world and in the home.

Today, women are almost half of the nation's workers. The dramatic changes in the work force are visible and easy to study because the government keeps careful records on it. The changes taking place in the home and in people's attitudes toward homemaking are harder to study because they occur behind closed doors. The government does not collect statistics on how husbands and wives divide household chores. The information must be gleaned from time-use studies, polls, and proprietary surveys. But the social change taking place in the home today is just as revolutionary as the change that took place outside the home in the past two decades. The baby-boom generation is at its leading edge.

CHAPTER 5

THE NEW CONSUMERS

More than 80% of baby boomers think about money often, and 60% often worry about money. Perhaps this is because baby boomers say that they would need $1.3 million dollars in their bank accounts before they felt rich, according to a survey by *Money* magazine. But nearly one-third of baby boomers saved no money in the past year.[1]

Over half of baby boomers say it would be a problem for them to pay an unexpected $1000 bill. But they are running up bills—87% have loans (including mortgages), and 69% have consumer loans.

The baby boom will spend a lot of money in the years ahead because middle-aged Americans are the biggest spenders. Each household headed by a 25- to 34-year-old spent an average of $21,500 in 1984. But each household headed by a 35- to 54-year-old spent much more—$28,000 in 1984, on average.[2]

Businesses are trying to figure out what the middle-aged baby boomers will buy. *Fortune* magazine wrote a wish-list for the generation that included furniture and appliances (especially high-priced furniture, microwaves, personal computers, and stereo TVs), cars (they like pricey European cars but can't afford them yet, says *Fortune*), food (more frozen foods, natural foods, more restaurant dinners), children's products (expensive stuff, to relieve their guilt about working all day), clothing (for the office, furs for after hours), and financial services (to finance their debts after they buy all these things).[3]

The baby boom is already the biggest consumer market in history. The generation's economic clout will grow as its income and spending grow. The people who shunned materialism when they were idealistic and penniless teenagers are getting more practical as their bank accounts grow in middle age. Practical means a car that always runs, a couch with new upholstery, a backyard deck, a down comforter for the winter, a basement playroom for the kids, a winter vacation.

THE HOUSE

The baby boomers spent $7100 on their homes in 1984, more than one-third of all their expenditures.[4]

This amount includes the mortgage or rent, the cost of electricity and other utilities, property taxes, furniture, and appliances.

As they get older, baby boomers can expect their housing costs to climb by about 25%, after adjusting for inflation, as they move out of their starter homes and into more spacious surroundings. But because their incomes will also rise, the share of expenditures that they devote to housing will remain at about one-third.

The boomers' housing costs will also climb as they upgrade their furniture and appliances. Householders aged 45 to 54 are the biggest spenders on appliances. By the turn of the century, appliance manufacturers should be in full production supplying the middle-aged with increasingly sophisticated household machines.

THE CAR

After housing, the next biggest expense for Americans is their cars. Baby-boom households spent $4600 on transportation in 1984 (one-fifth of all their spending).[5] Most of these households spent as much fueling and repairing their cars as they spent on the cars themselves—$2200 on cars, $1000 on gasoline and motor oil, and $1200 on repairs and other expenses. All of these costs will rise because the baby boomers will add to their car collection, buying higher-priced cars as their incomes grow. Households headed by 25- to 34-year-olds own an average of 1.8 cars. But households headed by 35- to 54-year-olds own more than two cars, on average.

FOOD

Food is the third biggest expense for Americans. Baby-boom households spent an average of $3100 on food in 1984.[6] But older householders spend even more on food because they have hungry children and teenagers to feed.

Almost half of every dollar Americans spend on food they spend at restaurants. The Department of Agriculture estimates that 41 cents of each food dollar goes for food eaten away from home, up from 27 cents in 1960.[7] A generation ago, dinner out was a treat; now it is taken for granted.

After adjusting for inflation, baby boomers will spend over 40% more on food in the next few decades as their families grow. In the grocery store, the boomers will boost sales of convenience foods (favored by busy, two-earner households), fresh vegetables, fruits, and fish (favored by those with relatively high incomes).

Baby boomers eat out twice a week, on average. In the past 20 years, the baby boom's taste for hamburgers and fries created the fast-food industry. But in the 1990s, the baby boomers from Pensacola, Florida, to Cheyenne, Wyoming, will patronize a different kind of restaurant. Even in middle America, traditional American food—the hotdog, the hamburger, steak and potatoes—will give way to Japanese, African, Thai, Brazilian, and other cuisines featuring exotic ingredients, preparations, and flavors.

Baby boomers' tastes are maturing. "Those who enjoy large portions served quickly are more likely to be the very young," says the *1984 Gallup Annual Report on Eating Out*.[8] Gallup finds that affluent baby boomers prefer theme and ethnic restaurants where they can experiment with new foods. Less affluent baby boomers and those with young children prefer family-style restaurants with a casual atmosphere and moderate prices.

Businesses that offer take-out and home-delivered foods will benefit the most from the middle-aged, home-oreinted baby boomers. Instead of spending a Saturday evening at a nice restaurant for entertainment, many people rent a movie, order take-out food or home delivery, and stay home. Going to the movies at home rather than in a theater is especially convenient for the parents of young children. The VCR combined with home-delivered foods may hurt the restaurant industry as more people decide to eat in. In fact, the revenues of white-tablecloth restaurants have been stagnating in 1986, according to *Nation's Restaurant News*, just when the demographics looked good.[9]

Instead of fighting the VCR, some restaurants are joining the revolution. Pizza Hut, Kentucky Fried Chicken, Arby's, Burger King, and many local restaurants now offer home delivery. Even grocery stores are experimenting with reestablishing this once-common service. In some metropolitan areas, forward-thinking entrepreneurs are grocery shopping for pay. Consumers call the shopping service in the morning with their grocery order. The service delivers the groceries to their homes in the afternoon for a fee, plus the cost of the groceries. In Detroit, even milkmen are making a comeback because busy, two-earner families demand con-

venience. The milkmen working for Detroit's Twin Pines
Dairy Farm are a convenience store on wheels, also selling baked goods and produce.

With more businesses literally knocking on the baby
boom's front doors, traditional retailing may suffer in the
coming years. Banking by computer, direct-mail, home
delivery, telephone ordering, and catalog shopping—all
of which appeal to the baby boom—take customers away
from the downtowns and the shopping malls.

ENTERTAINMENT

The home will be the focal point for entertainment
in the 1990s because technological change is strengthen-
ing its role in people's lives. Baby-boom households
spent an average of $1100 on entertainment in 1984, in-
cluding fees and admissions to parks, movies, plays, and
other events, as well as the cost of televisions, stereos,
VCRs, and other electronic entertainment equipment.[10]
The baby boomers' entertainment costs will be one-third
greater a decade from now, after adjusting for inflation,
as their incomes grow. People aged 35 to 44 are the biggest spenders on entertainment.

VCRs, home computers, compact disk stereo systems, large-screen TVs, and pocket-sized TVs—none of
these products was widely available before 1980, yet now
they are changing the nature of entertainment.

In 1985, movie box office revenues fell 8% and ticket
sales fell 12%.[11] While the motion picture industry experiences cyclical downturns in box office receipts, the
latest drop may be the first sign of permanent change.

The $3.7 billion Americans spent at the movies in 1985 was only slightly more than the $3.3 billion they spent renting or buying videocassettes for their VCRs. In 1986, videocassette revenues topped movie revenues for the first time; the gap between movie theater revenues and videocassette revenues will grow larger each year. By 1995, predicts one forecaster, revenues from the sale and rental of prerecorded videocassettes will be three times those from movie admissions.[12]

In 1950, the average American aged 10 to 39 (the prime moviegoers) went to the movies 38 times a year. By 1970, people in that age group were going to only eight movies a year as television competed with movies for people's leisure time.[13] Since 1970, moviegoing has held steady, but it may head down again. Between 1984 and 1985, the number of 10- to 39-year-olds who went to the movies declined. The new home technologies available to Americans, combined with the aging of the baby-boom generation, are dramatically changing the leisure industry.

"The videocassette recorder has re-legitimized the television set as a center of activity for adult socializing," notes *Adweek*.[14] "Somehow, a rented movie counts as an evening out." The VCR is bringing the baby boom back home.

In 1985, there were 20,000 movie screens in the United States, the most this country may ever have. In the coming decades, theater owners will transform the small, cramped theaters of today into larger ones that lure people out of their living rooms by offering sumptuous surroundings, good sound systems, hors d'oeuvres, and babysitting services.

The new home technologies offer people more choice. The proliferation of cable television stations and the introduction of the VCR have made television more diverse, with programs geared to many interests. Forty-seven percent of American households are wired for cable, and 55% will be by 1990, according to Grey Advertising.[15] Because of competition with videocassette rentals, cable movie channels are likely to offer more first-run movies in the years ahead. The retail stores that rent prerecorded videocassettes may become to the movie industry what libraries are to the book industry. People will watch first-run movies on cable; they will rent the movies they missed from the local store.

In the 1990s, the VCR will be as common as the television in American homes. It will be a bigger entertainment medium than movies or network television. Already, the network share of the television audience has fallen to 73%, down from 89% a decade ago as cable television and prerecorded tapes compete with the networks for viewers. By 1990, only two-thirds of the television audience will be watching network TV, according to the advertising agency BBD&O.[16] The rest of the audience will be watching public television, recording programs with their VCRs, or viewing rented movies, cable television, and movie channels.

Other more sophisticated technologies will introduce entirely new forms of entertainment into the home. One of them is the interactive compact disk. By plugging a compact disk into an audiovisual system, people will be able to experience and even interact with another place—a fantasy world perhaps, or even a foreign part of the real world. The streets of Paris will stretch out ahead of them on their large-screen television monitors.

On their stationary exercise bicycles, they can bicycle down the streets, turn at any intersection, and even stop at a store, walk in, and look around. They are in Paris while still in their own living rooms.

The baby boomers will be the first Americans to adopt these new technologies. Already, the baby boom has transformed television from a passive viewing technology into an active one, according to *Adweek*, because baby boomers are comfortable with electronics.[17]

Even the nation's home builders can bank on the baby boom's love of technology. Ryan Homes, the nation's fourth largest home builder, is installing computerized control centers in its new homes. These centers, manufactured by General Electric, are called ''Homeminders.'' Homeminder allows the homeowner to schedule and control lights, appliances, furnaces, and air conditioners, activating them remotely by telephone. According to Ryan Homes president Steve Smith, the baby boomers are busy with work and family, familiar with electronics, and willing to pay to guard their leisure time.[18]

LEISURE TIME

The average American has 18 hours of leisure each week, eight hours less than ten years ago, according to a Louis Harris & Associates Survey.[19] The baby-boom generation skews the national statistics as it finds its free time in increasingly short supply.

Though they have less of it than the average American, most baby boomers treat leisure as a necessity. Leisure is no longer something that must be earned through hard work, according to *Adweek's* Maria Fisher. "A generation of Americans has come to see leisure as a birthright, even if the way they spend it seems anything but leisurely."[20]

Young adults and the elderly have the most leisure time. Neither group has to shoulder many of the responsibilities that burden the middle-aged: young adults don't have family and home ownership responsibilities, and most of the elderly are retired. People aged 18 to 29 enjoy 19 hours of leisure a week, according to the Louis Harris Survey, while those aged 65 and older have 25 hours of leisure a week.

People aged 30 to 49 have only 16 hours of leisure a week because of their work and family responsibilities. No wonder so many baby boomers feel rushed. Sixty-two percent of unmarried people report having time on their hands, compared to only one-third of parents raising children, according to a United Media Enterprises Report.[21] The baby boom's leisure lifestyle—single and unencumbered—has become a married and harried lifestyle as it juggles work and family.

Most singles look for excitement during their leisure hours. Most couples would rather spend their free time with their families. Only 20% of singles spend their leisure hours at home, compared to 46% of dual-career parents.

Despite Americans' shrinking leisure time and television habit, reading is gaining in popularity. Twenty-one percent of Americans are currently reading a book, up from 14% in 1955.[22] The well-educated baby-boom generation is behind the increasing popularity of books.

People aged 35 to 49—ironically, those with the least leisure time—are most likely to read. Because the baby boom is entering this age group, the next few decades should be good ones for the book industry. The Book Industry Study Group reports that Americans buy an average of six books a year, up from three in 1970. By 1990, they will buy eight a year, the Study Group projects.[23] The interests of the baby boom will dictate the bestseller lists of the 1990s and beyond.

In the 1970s, the baby boom tested the adult waters, searching for identity. Books about psychology and self-exploration, such as *Zen and the Art of Motorcycle Maintenance* and *Be Here Now*, were the hot sellers. As the baby boom aged into its late 20s and early 30s, when career building is important, management books were sure sellers. *In Search of Excellence, The One-Minute Manager*, and *Iacocca* took the market by storm. Now the baby boom is buying homes and raising children. No wonder a book called *House* was on the bestseller list in 1985. As baby-boom lives come to center increasingly on the home, family themes will dominate the next two decades of nonfiction.

People aged 35 to 49 are the biggest buyers of nonfiction. Because of this, the Gallup Organization predicts that reference and instruction books will be popular as the baby boom teaches its children about the world. Autobiography, biography, history, and religious books should flourish. The aging of the baby boom also promises to be good for historical fiction, mystery and suspense, and action and adventure novels. But humor, science fiction, and romance novels could lose market share.[24]

Magazines, too, are benefiting from more readers. The baby-boom generation determines which magazines will succeed and which will not. In the last 15 years, the generation graduated from *Seventeen* magazine to *Savvy*, from *Road and Track* to *House and Garden*, and from *Rolling Stone* to *Businessweek*. People subscribe to magazines that tell them something about their lives; as their lives change, magazines that once interested them lose appeal while those that bored them become more relevant.

The median age of magazine readers reflects how people's interests change as they age. For people in their 20s, the popular magazines include *Bride, American Baby*, and *Road and Track*, according to Mediamark Research, Inc., of New York.[25] In their early 30s, people read *Working Mother, Ms., Outdoor Life*, and *Sports Illustrated*. In their late 30s, people like *Fortune, Businessweek, New Shelter*, and *Food and Wine*. In their early 40s, people read *Bon Appetit, Gourmet, Country Living, Golf Magazine*, and *House and Garden*. And by their late 40s, Americans putter around with *Travel/Holiday, Sunset, Prevention*, and *Organic Gardening*.

Rock magazines took off when the baby boom was in its teens; business magazines flourished when the generation entered its 30s. In the 1990s, the magazines that address the concerns of the new homemaker will do well. But the home-oriented magazines that appeal to more traditional homemakers, such as *Family Circle* and *Woman's Day*, may lose readers unless they change their approach, because their traditional audience is disappearing.

The baby boom one day will move beyond its absorbing interest in home and family—sometime after the

turn of the century. When the generation retires, magazines devoted to travel, tourism, gardening, birdwatch-
ing, and healthy living will be chock-full of advertisers
reaching out to the baby boom.

GOING OUT

Despite their lack of leisure time, baby boomers are
more likely than older people to go out—over 90% of
boomers go to the movies each year, and more than two-
thirds go to plays. Over half attend popular music concerts and visit art museums.[26]

The college-educated are much more likely than the
less educated to attend arts events. Seventy-eight percent of college graduates visit an art museum at least
once a year, for example, compared to only 46% of people who went no further than high school. The aging of
the well-educated baby-boom generation bodes well for
American arts in the next few decades. The arts also
should get a boost from the growing generosity of the
generation.

Each year, 89% of Americans give money away, according to a national survey by Yankelovich, Skelly, and
White, Inc.[27] Among givers, the middle-aged are the
most charitable. Baby-boom households gave away $368
in 1984, including contributions to their churches—a
lowly sum in comparison to the charity of older householders, who gave away more than $1000.[28]

But in the decades ahead, baby-boom households
will give away three times as much money as they do

today. The charity of the baby boom should help churches the most, since nearly half of all charitable dollars go to religious groups. But social, political, and artistic organizations that depend on charity should also prosper during the affluent decades ahead. For example, people aged 30 to 49 and college graduates are most likely to give money to the arts.[29]

Eighty-three percent of the funding for charitable organizations comes from individuals; the rest comes from corporations and the government.[30] Because of this, communities across the country should find themselves infused with funds for the arts in the next 20 years. This could spur an American renaissance of sorts which might include more live theater, community concerts, and traveling art exhibits.

People are more likely to give away their money than their time. Only 48% of Americans volunteer for community organizations; these volunteers donate an average of 18 hours a month of their time, and most of that goes to their churches.[31]

The baby boom's turn is coming, because middle-aged Americans are most likely to volunteer. While only about 43% of 18- to 24-year-olds donate their time for a cause, fully 54% of 35- to 49-year-olds volunteer—the highest proportion among all age groups. Volunteering rises with education, too—65% of college graduates volunteer. As the baby-boom generation ages into its 40s, American communities may discover many more people willing to lend a hand. Though the baby boomers' lesiure time will be in short supply, a larger chunk of what little leisure they have will go to worthy causes.

VACATIONS

Spending on vacation homes and hotels will be one of the most rapidly growing expenditure categories in the next few decades, according to Shearson Lehman Economics, because the baby boom will travel more and in more style.[32]

More than two out of three Americans travel more than 100 miles from their homes each year, according to the U.S. Travel Data Center. Two-thirds of these trips are vacations; the rest are business and personal trips.[33]

The people most likely to travel are college graduates and those with household incomes of $30,000 or more. The aging of the baby-boom generation, its educational level, and its rising income all point to a travel boom. The baby boom will reshape the travel industry to suit its needs.

"Ten years ago the typical trip to Europe averaged three weeks," says Jean Epping, president of the American Society of Travel Agents. "Today that average is 10 days."[34] Cruises are also getting shorter to accommodate working baby boomers who can't leave their jobs for weeks at a time. A *Wall Street Journal*/NBC News poll found that 28% of working couples who vacationed in the past year took a shorter trip than five years earlier. "Working couples are transforming the traditional two-week vacation by taking shorter trips, extended weekends or taking spouses along on business trips," reports the *Journal*.[35]

Nevertheless, Americans are vacationing more than they used to. Three-fourths of Americans took a week-long vacation in 1985, up from only 56% in 1960, according to a Market Opinion Research study of Americans' vacation habits.[36] Eighty-five percent of Americans took a long-weekend vacation in 1985. Fifty-three percent of baby boomers took at least four long-weekend trips during the year.

Most Americans (57%) prefer taking several long-weekend vacations throughout the year rather than a single two- or three-week vacation, according to a survey taken by R. H. Bruskin for the Marriott Corporation.[37] Those most in favor of weekend trips are people aged 35 to 49, dual-career couples, and high-income households.

The baby boom is finding alternatives to the two-week family vacation because dual careers make it doubly hard to get away for long. For the next few decades, the quick foreign trip, the short cruise, and the weekend jaunt will reshape American travel. Terrorism will not dampen the baby boomers' enthusiasm for the open road, though it will determine which countries the boomers are likely to visit and which they will avoid.

FITNESS AND SPORTS

Baby boomers regularly take part in an average of 4.5 physical activities a year, such as swimming, aerobics, dancing, camping, or fishing. Older people take part in only 2.4 activities on a regular basis.[38] But as the baby boomers get older, they may not trade in their sweatsuits for leisure suits, according to results from the

National Recreation Survey (NRS) of the Department of the Interior.

By comparing the results of the latest NRS survey with one taken 20 years earlier, University of Maryland professor John P. Robinson finds that older Americans are getting more active, no matter what their age.[39] Americans aged 45 and older in the 1980s did more bicycling, camping, hiking, tennis, and skiing than did older people 20 years ago.

Robinson found that people who were active in 1965 were just as active in 1982. Fifteen percent of people aged 25 to 44 bicycled in 1965, for example. In 1982, the participation rate for these same people—now aged 45 to 64—was 16%. Apparently, exercise becomes a lifelong habit.

The NRS findings suggest that the sports baby boomers enjoy today they will also enjoy tomorrow. Today, 37% of baby boomers bicycle, 65% swim, 40% fish, 30% camp, and 31% run. Twenty percent of baby boomers play tennis, 13% golf, 7% sail, 13% hunt, 17% hike, 8% go downhill skiing and 4% ski cross-country.[40] Twelve percent do aerobics.[41]

Some sports grew in popularity over the past few decades, while others have declined because of changes in the age structure of the population, people's lifestyles, and technology. For example, downhill skiing did not become an important sport until ski lifts were perfected. Improved technologies have also helped tennis, camping, cross-country skiing, bicycling, and many other sports.

Bicycling has gained dramatically in popularity, tennis participation has tripled since 1960, and the number of campers has doubled.[42] Jogging was not even included in the 1960 recreational survey because it was such an insignificant activity. Snow skiing has quadrupled in participation since 1960. The growing popularity of skiing, however, may have hurt other winter sports activities, like ice skating and sledding, which lost popularity since the 1960s.

Participation in some recreational activities changed little over the past 20 years: picnicking, sightseeing, fishing, hunting, water-skiing, and horseback riding hold a steady place in Americans' hearts.

As the baby boom gets older and earns more money, costly recreational activities, such as sailing, motorboating, and golfing should gain in popularity. Cities across the country may be pressured to develop public golf courses. More man-made lakes, complete with marinas, may dot the American landscape.

Some leisure activities may not do so well in the years ahead. Forty percent of Americans attended an outdoor sporting event in 1982–1983, according to the NRS, almost double the participation rate of 1960.[43] But the audience for live sporting events may level off in the 1990s. Among people aged 25 to 39, 44% were spectators at an outdoor sporting event in 1982–1983, compared with 36% of 40- to 59-year-olds and 16% of people aged 60 and older.

Among ten spectator sports analyzed by Simmons Market Research Bureau, baseball is the only one that appeals more to the middle-aged than to the young.[44] Baseball already is the most popular American sport—

21 million Americans went to a professional baseball game in 1985. In comparison, only 10 million Americans went to a professional football game. Baseball's popularity is likely to grow in the 1990s as the baby boom enters middle age. But other sporting events, even football, may find their live audience shrinking as the number of young adults in the population declines.

DEBTS AND ASSETS

In the 1990s, the baby boom will earn enough money to save money. Financial savings should be one of the most rapidly growing "expenditure" categories in the decades ahead, according to Shearson Lehman Economics.

Today the baby boom is more likely to spend money than to save. The median balance in the checking accounts of baby boomers was $327 in 1984.[45] Among the 65% of baby boomers who had savings accounts, the median balance was $901, according to the Census Bureau.

Households headed by 25- to 44-year-olds are most likely to be in debt, according to the Federal Reserve Board. In 1983, 77% of householders aged 25 to 34 owed a median of $2300 in consumer loans, while 79% of households headed by 35- to 44-year-olds owed a median of $3000.[46] The 1980s and 1990s should be a good decade for the financial markets, as boomers borrow to buy. In 1984, consumer installment debt rose 20%, and in 1985 it rose another 18%, spurred by the borrowing of the baby boom.[47]

Eight out of ten baby boomers own credit cards, according to a 1985 *Money* magazine survey, and 11% own premium or gold cards.[48] More than one-third charged over $1000 on their cards in the past 12 months. But a mere 22% of baby boomers pay their full credit card balance each month. Because of this, baby boomers have almost as many debts as they have assets, but that's about to change.

The net worth (assets minus debts) of householders younger than age 35 was just $5800 in 1984, according to the Census Bureau.[49] Net worth rises sharply with age as people pay off their debts and begin to save money. The median net worth of 35- to 44-year-olds was $35,600 in 1984; for 45- to 54-year-olds it was $56,800, and it peaked for 55- to 64-year-olds at $73,700.

Overall, 40% of baby-boom households own a home, with a median home equity of $17,600. Eighty-eight percent own a car (median equity, $3300); 10% have their own business (median equity, $2600); and 10% have an IRA or Keogh account (median balance, $2500). During the next 20 years, the assets of baby boomers will become more valuable. Growing the most in value will be their homes, as they pay off their mortgage debt.

In fact, the home is the biggest asset of most Americans, accounting for an average of 41% of net worth. The baby boom's parents saw the value of this asset grow enormously in the past few decades, as their children spurred demand for housing and drove up prices. Because of this, 43% of Americans think that investing in real estate is one of the best ways to get rich, according to *Money* magazine—second only to working hard.[50] But many baby boomers may be in for a surprise. In most areas of the country, home values are likely to rise no more than the inflation rate because the small baby-bust generation will be buying homes in the 1990s. Housing demand will drop, and consequently housing prices will stabilize.

The baby boom is used to spending money because that was a good investment strategy in the 1970s, when double-digit inflation and escalating real estate prices meant that those who spent money saved money later. Today, with inflation down, spending is the wrong way to make ends meet. The baby boom must relearn the ins and outs of finance. In the decades ahead, those who pay off their loans and build their savings have the greatest chance of achieving affluence.

Now that double-digit returns are few and far between, the baby boom is beginning to dabble in the stock market. The boomers first hit the market on September 23, 1985, when the Dow Jones Industrial Average began its historic rise from just below 1300 to over 1900 in nine months. Few analysts could explain it. But a page one story in *The Wall Street Journal* cited the aging of the American population.

"As the postwar baby boomers enter middle age, they have become more conservative financially and politically," noted the *Journal*.[51] According to the article, the baby boomers are now concerned about families and finances, and this has bullish implications for the financial markets. Some analysts "anticipate a golden age lasting into the 1990s." There will be healthy corrections, of course, but the stock market should continue to rise for a decade or more since the baby boom is heading into the middle-aged years of spending. This should boost corporate profits, and as profits go so goes the stock market.

The number of people owning stock jumped from 30 million in 1980 to fully 47 million in 1985, a 56% rise, according to a survey by the New York Stock Exchange.[52] The median age of stockholders fell from 52 in 1975 to 44 in 1985. The first baby boomers will turn 44 in 1990.

Twenty-two percent of baby boomers owned stock in 1984, including those who own stock through company plans.[53] Between 1983 and 1985, 77% of new investors in the stock market were aged 21 to 44. Among the new investors, women account for 57%. The typical new investor, in fact, is a woman aged 34, married, working in a professional or technical job, with a portfolio of $2200 and a household income of $35,000 a year.

Most baby boomers, however, will not risk their savings in the stock market. The most important investment goal for people younger than age 35 is not to lose money. But the middle-aged aren't content just to stay even. The most important investment goal among people aged 35 to 54 is income growth, according to the research firm Market Facts, Inc.[54] One in five people aged 35 to 54 is willing to take more than a little financial risk to see income growth. As the baby boom inflates this middle-aged group in the next two decades, a greater proportion of Americans will take risks as they look for another fledgling Apple Computer, hoping for the big win, the $1.3 million that will make them feel rich.

FUN MONEY

After the monthly mortgage check is written and the refrigerator is stocked with groceries, most people don't have much money left. But one-third of American households do have money left over—this is what some people call fun money. The government statisticians call this "discretionary" income—dollars that people can spend on whatever they want because their bills are paid.

The percentage of households with discretionary income rises as people get older and earn more money. This means that a growing share of baby boomers can look forward to fun money in the future.

To calculate how much money is "discretionary," the Census Bureau and the Consumer Research Center of the Conference Board estimate the average expenditures of households.[55] Those households with an after-tax income at least 30% greater than average expenditures they define as having discretionary income.

The average before-tax income of baby-boom households with discretionary income ranged from $42,000 to $52,000 in 1983. For these lucky households, the average amount of fun money available to them ranged from $7700 to $10,100. With these dollars, baby boomers buy such things as computers, second cars, European vacations, or remodeled kitchens.

Households with two earners are much more likely to have discretionary income than those with just one earner. Forty-six percent of two-income couples have discretionary income, versus just 32% of the households in which the husband is the sole breadwinner. Fifty-two percent of households headed by college graduates have discretionary income, as do fully 61% of households headed by people who have been to graduate school.

The college-educated, two-income, middle-aged, married couples of the 1990s and 2000s will find them-

selves with unprecedented spending power. Four out of
ten baby-boom households will have fun money to play
with, an average of $10,000 a year per household. Busi-
nesses that focused on youth for the past 30 years are
quickly changing course, creating products and services
that will provide the middle-aged baby boom with toys
of which it will never tire.

BUSINESS AND THE BABY BOOM

American businesses will have to get to know these
middle-aged baby-boom consumers if they want to take
advantage of their buying power. The baby boom lives
differently and buys differently than previous generations of middle-aged.

The baby boomers have a globalistic view of the
American economy. They will buy imports instead of
domestics if they think the domestics don't stack up.
Only 48% of baby boomers believe that American-made
products are of better quality than imports, according to
the American Society for Quality Control.[56] In contrast,
two out of three people aged 50 and older believe that
American-made products are the best. The college-
educated and those with high incomes are least likely to
believe American products are of high quality. If American businesses want the baby boom's dollar, they will
have to convince the generation that the ''made in
America'' stamp symbolizes the high standards it once
did.

Baby-boom men and women live alike. As their roles
merge, product advertising must appeal to both sexes.
Both men and women buy household cleaning products,

children's products, cars, and office products, for example. Advertisers should speak to both or risk missing a large market.

Many baby boomers experiment with new things—whether it's exotic foods in a restaurant, new technologies in the home, or new ways of buying things. Half of baby boomers bought something through the mail in the past 12 months, according to Mediamark Research, Inc.[57] Six out of ten baby boomers told *Money* magazine that they would feel comfortable banking by computer.[58] The baby boomers are likely to do more shopping at home in the decades ahead because they value their spare time and they own the technologies (such as computers and cable hook-ups) that make this possible. Some analysts predict that by the mid-1990s, one-fourth to one-third of all retail sales in the United States will take place out-of-store through such things as television shopping channels, 800 numbers, and mail order catalogs.[59] If retail stores want to keep the baby boomers as customers, they will have to pay close attention to their needs.

The baby boom is less formal than older generations of Americans. The clothing styles of the baby boom reveal just how informal it is. Between 1980 and 1984, when the number of men working in professional and managerial jobs increased by 1 million, the sales of men's business suits stagnated. According to a Roper survey, ''most Americans couldn't care less about dressing for success.'' In fact, says Roper, ''informality is the order of the day for the majority of the nation's workers.''[60] Few men wear a suit and tie to work. Even among men with salaries of $35,000 or more, only 22% always wear a suit to work and only 31% always wear a tie. Just 15%

of high-income women—those who earn $35,000 a year or more—wear a dress or suit to work every day, according to Roper. Sixty-four percent of these high earners wear slacks to work every day. Dr. Spock told the parents of the baby boom that they should dress to please others. The baby boom dresses to please itself.

The baby boom hungers after, and is willing to pay for, experiences. The Stanford Research Institute's Values, Attitudes, and Lifestyles (VALS) program, which tracks people's changing beliefs and behavior, has identified a new kind of consumer emerging as the baby boom ages. Instead of buying in order to own things as people did in the 1950s and 1960s, the baby boom buys to experience something—the feel of Europe, the thrill of mountain climbing, the drama of the 1812 Overture, the satisfaction of a turbo-charged engine. "From the point of view of the consumer," says Stanford Research Institute researcher James Ogilvy, "the real meaning of the information revolution lies in the growth of the experience industry: not a computer in every home, but an increasingly wide range of experiences."[61]

Many American companies are selling products by appealing to the baby boom's thirst for experience. Banana Republic, a clothing company owned by The Gap, designs its catalogs like exotic travel guides. Pier 1, a chain of stores that sold teenaged baby boomers Indian-print bedspreads and brass do-dahs in the 1960s, is now outfitting the homes of middle-aged baby boomers with furniture and accessories in the 1980s. The company uses the experiential sell to lure customers to its products. When customers browse or buy at Pier 1, they learn something about the products from the instructional cards positioned around the store.[62] The travel industry also uses educational experience as a selling point for vacation packages: Cruise the Black Sea and study architecture; learn French in Paris; discover sailing at Club Med.

Learning fulfills the baby boom's desire for experience. It is also the ultimate in instant gratification. Many baby boomers want to learn a skill, or how something is done, or how people live in another country, without investing a lifetime in it. Two weeks at Club Med or six minutes perusing a clothing catalog can help them learn—and experience—something new.

CHAPTER 6

THE NEW BELIEVERS

For almost two decades, the nation has held its breath, waiting for the baby boom to make its mark in politics. It hasn't happened yet. Ever since Eugene McCarthy ran in the Presidential primaries of 1968—the year that the oldest baby boomer turned 22—the country has expected more out of the baby boom than it cared to give. In the election of 1972, when the oldest baby boomer was 26, all eyes were on George McGovern—could he pull it off with the baby boom's help? But the baby boom didn't deliver.

Though some boomers were old enough to vote as far back as 1968, few did. This failure is not unique to the baby-boom generation. Young adults are less likely to vote than older people. Because of this, young people make up a smaller share of voters than of the population in general.

Though the baby boom made up over 40% of the voting-age population in 1984, it accounted for less than 40% of voters.[1] People aged 45 and older constituted 42% of the voting age population, but fully 48% of voters.

"It may seem that the political impact of the baby boomers peaked in the late 1960s and early 1970s, before they were old enough to vote," says Jane Newitt, director of demographic research for the Hudson Institute. But, she says, "the 1970s was the decade of the young nonvoter."[2]

In 1980 and 1984, only about 40% of 18- to 24-year-olds voted, compared to 58% of 25- to 44-year-olds, and about 70% of people aged 45 and older.[3] Americans aren't likely to vote until they have something to protect—and young people don't have much to protect. As the baby boom gets older, however, a larger proportion of the generation will vote.

Another fact of political life also promises to make the baby boom a political power to reckon with: In the Presidential election of 1984, 79% of Americans with a college diploma cast a ballot versus 68% of people with some college experience, 59% of high school graduates, and 44% of high school dropouts. Nothing draws people to the polls more than an education.

The aging of the baby boom, combined with its educational level, means that the generation will have its first major impact on the nation's politics in the Presidential election of 1992. Almost 50 million baby boomers will vote in that year, millions more than in 1984; they will represent nearly half of all voters. The disproportionate power of the baby boom in the voting booth will continue well into the next century. Even in the presidential election of 2020, when the youngest baby boomer is 56, the generation will still dominate the nation's electorate.

If the baby boomers get together on the issues, they will be the most potent political force in the nation's history.

BABY-BOOM POLITICS

Though the baby-boom generation has not yet had an impact in the voting booth, it is changing American politics. The political system no longer revolves around one axis, but two.

The baby boom is both conservative and liberal. The generation has become economically conservative with age, but remains socially liberal on many issues.

Ronald Reagan is a conservative both economically and socially. Yet many baby boomers voted for Reagan in 1980 and 1984 for economic reasons. In fact, the baby boom disagreed with most of Reagan's social agenda—such as his opposition to the Equal Rights Amendment—but, tired of the stagnant economy of the 1970s, they were more willing to vote for a social conservative than an economic liberal. They wanted control over the nation's economy.

But another Ronald Reagan will not satisfy the baby boom voting block in the election years ahead. The kind of politician who finally will win the presidency will straddle the line between conservative and liberal. Already this kind of politician made inroads in the primaries: John Anderson in 1980; Gary Hart in 1984.

The baby boomers have a social conscience: They believe in the equality of women, they are open to change, and they are uncomfortable with the gulf that exists between their values and their lifestyles, according to Republican political consultant Lee Atwater. "Candidates who understand this gulf and try to make values and lifestyles work together for this group are going to do very well," says Atwater.[4]

Democrat Pat Caddell, president of Cambridge Survey Research, defines the baby boom's social conscience: "This is a generation with a collective sense that they can do great things, yet they are leading a life right now that's fairly mundane in terms of changing the world. Neither political party has been able to reach this generation in a way that would allow it—and its aspiration to change the world—to become a central power force. The one that does will likely be the majority party for the rest of the century."[5]

MORE CONSERVATIVE

The baby boom is more conservative today than it used to be. This is what happens to people as they grow older.

In 1975, 46% of people aged 20 to 29 (the oldest baby
boomers) called themselves liberals, according to an analysis of the General Social Survey of the National Opinion Research Center in Chicago.[6] But by 1985, only 29%
of 30- to 39-year-olds said they were liberals, a loss of 17
percentage points. Though the older baby boomers are
still more likely to be liberal than older Americans, they
are not as liberal as they used to be. They are even less
liberal than people aged 30 to 39 were in 1975.

Baby boomers in their 30s in 1985 are more likely to
identify themselves as conservatives than as liberals—
34% say they are conservatives, up from only 19% of 20-
to 29-year-olds in 1975. The "moderate" faction increased slightly during the decade, from 35% of 20- to
29-year-olds in 1975 to 38% of 30- to 39-year-olds in 1985.

Among the younger baby boomers, those aged 22 to
29 in 1985, 31% consider themselves liberals, a larger
proportion than among their older brothers and sisters.
This is contrary to the conservative reputation that younger baby boomers have. Twenty-nine percent of the
younger boomers called themselves conservatives in
1985, and 39% labeled themselves moderates.

People in their 40s and 50s tend to be the most conservative. These are the ages when salary, jobs, housing, and children are of primary importance, making the
middle-aged cautious. Older people are less conservative
than the middle-aged—26% of people aged 60 and older
call themselves "liberals," compared to just 19% of people in their 50s and 22% of people in their 40s.

In the next two decades, the baby boom is likely to
become even more conservative. This doesn't mean,

however, that the baby boomers will be traditional conservatives. In fact, on specific issues the baby boom is staunchly liberal. Only 16% of baby boomers aged 30 to 39 want to spend more money on defense. Only 4% think the United States spends too much on the environment. Less than half believe welfare spending is excessive. Seventy-seven percent believe in gun control.

Surprisingly, however, 66% believe the United States spends too much on foreign aid, 82% favor capital punishment, and 86% think the courts are too easy on criminals.

THE POLITICS OF THE FUTURE

The baby boom's tolerance of diversity and its acceptance of individual rights will mold American politics for the next 40 years. And as college graduates become a larger share of voters, they will change government policy, according to the Hudson Institute's Jane Newitt. Highly educated voters want consistency across issues. They watch how a politician votes on a range of issues—such as gun control and defense spending—rather than on just one issue.

In the next decade, the United States will enter a political era dominated by baby boomers who "will favor legislators who seek to expand individual opportunities and environmental protection," according to Newitt.[7] The boomers will also "reward those who want to decentralize government's social roles, control the tax bite, stimulate economic growth, and maintain military preparedness."

The 1990s may, in fact, be more liberal than the 1970s or 1980s. But liberalism has a new meaning, says Newitt—it is "a receptivity to change." This openness to change, she suggests, will define the baby boom's politics for decades to come.

RELIGIOUS REVIVAL

Religion was in its heyday in the 1950s when the baby boomers were born. Church membership increased rapidly and religious feeling, according to the polls, was high. In fact, this level of activity has never been surpassed. But some observers question the religiousness of the 1950s, claiming that millions of Americans were going to church because it was "the thing to do," says George Gallup, Jr.[8]

Going to church is no longer "the thing to do," but millions of Americans still go. Despite the revival of religion in the past few years, however, religious activity remains below what it was 30 years ago.

In 1957, 69% of Americans felt that religion had an increasing influence on American life. The percentage of people who say religion's influence is increasing fell to a low of 14% in 1969 and 1970, then began to climb. In 1985, 48% of Americans believed that religion's influence was increasing.[9]

Three out of four Americans said that religion was very important in their lives in 1952. Just over half of Americans say that today—56% in 1985. But fully 95% of Americans believe in God or a universal spirit, a proportion that has been stable for the past 40 years. Younger people are less likely to believe in God than older people, however, and more educated people are also less likely to believe in God, says Gallup.

Sixty-eight percent of Americans belonged to a church or synagogue in 1985, close to the 73% of 1952. Only 40% of Americans attend church each week, however.

People's religious feelings change as they get older. Young adults often reject religion, then go back to church after they marry and have children. In its middle age, the baby boom is rediscovering religion. The baby boomers are slower to do this than previous generations, because they are marrying and having children later in life. In addition, the baby boomers are more educated than older Americans, making them less likely to hold religious beliefs.

About half of baby boomers are Protestant, 30% are Catholic, and 2% are Jewish. Twelve percent have no religious preference, compared to only 4% of people aged 50 and older.

GROWING SPLIT

Catholics make up a growing share of Americans because of the immigration of Hispanics into the country. Baptists are growing in dominance in the South, and the percentage of people with no religion is on the rise, says Tom W. Smith of the National Opinion Research Center.[10]

Smith traces the growth or decline of religious denominations to demographic change. Moderate religions (which he defines as Lutherans, Methodists, Presbyterians, and Espiscopalians) are losing ground. Presbyterians, he says, comprise 7% of the people born before 1907, but only 3% of those born between 1958 and 1965. Just as the middle-income class is losing members to the lower and upper classes, so the moderate religions are losing members to the growing ranks of the nonreligious and the fundamentalists.

Smith predicts that the percentage of Americans at either end of the religious spectrum (fundamentalists at the one extreme and the nonreligious at the other) will increase. This will intensify the split among Americans in values and attitudes, Smith says.

Only 9% of Americans are Protestant fundamentalists, but the group is gaining adherents through conversion and also because of the higher fertility of fundamentalist families. Twelve percent of people born between 1958 and 1965 claim to be fundamentalists, versus only 8% of those born in the early part of the century. Because the number of fundamentalists is growing, these groups are making waves in American culture.

But the fundamentalists will not be able to turn back the clock, because they fail to recognize that the new economic rules of life demand a new way of life. ''The Religious Right has captured the attention of the media, and the movement may even win some legislative and judicial victories in the short run,'' says Paul D. Kleppner, director of the Social Science Research Institute at Northern Illinois University. ''But its success is likely to be fleeting because the movement swims against the tide of social and attitudinal change.''[11]

LOOKING FOR ANSWERS

In 1973, *Time* magazine asked whether God was dead. That year marked a low point in religious belief, in part because the baby boom was in its teenage and early adult years—the years when people reject what their parents taught them and look for other answers. The baby boom's rejection of traditional religion occurred simultaneously (and not coincidentally) with a rise in religious cults and exotic religious practices.

Now that the baby boomers are having children, many of them are returning to religious tradition to give their children a set of beliefs. But the generation's new lifestyles mean that it needs something different from religion than its parents do. The baby boomers need reassurance that the unique course they steer through turbulent waters will not harm their families; they need to feel that they are OK in an ever-changing world.

Americans' religious fervor may never surpass what it was in the 1950s because the country is more diverse today. No one religion can dominate the culture as Protestant Christianity did 30 years ago. The Catholic church is gaining adherents because of the growth of the Hispanic population; Hinduism and Buddhism are also gaining ground today because of the immigration of Asians into the United States. Fundamentalists are growing, but so are the nonreligious who outnumber them.

Religion will play a central role in the lives of most baby boomers, and in the social and economic choices the country makes in the next few decades. The debate over the proper place of religion in a democratic society is likely to continue.

OLD AGE

CHAPTER 7

THE NEW OLD

If midlife is the age at which people have lived half their lives, then the baby boom is there. For men, midlife is age 37, when they have an equal number of years of life remaining. For women, midlife is age 40, when they have 40 years of life left. The middle age of the baby boom will stretch for nearly three decades. By 2011, the first baby boomers will turn 65. Then the generation will find out what it's like to be old.

The older people get, the older "old age" becomes. Old age starts at age 63, say people in their 20s. People in their 40s say that old age starts at 70. For the elderly (people aged 65 and older), old age starts at age 75.[1]

If old age is defined as the age at which people have an average of only ten more years of life, then it begins at age 73 for men and 78 for women, say demographers Jacob S. Siegel and Cynthia M. Taeuber.[2] But if old age begins with retirement, then people reach old age sooner. Sixty-five is no longer the traditional age of retirement. Now it is 62, according to the federal government's General Accounting Office.[3] The office's estimates are based on the age at which half of workers are drawing on their pensions.

The oldest baby boomers will turn 55 in 2001. For some, that year will mark the beginning of retirement. Though most baby boomers will have to wait to age 67 before they receive full Social Security benefits, this won't keep them from retiring early if they can afford to because the generation is as serious about its leisure as it is about its work. After working hard for decades, the baby boom will be ready for a change.

Two decades ago, over half of men were still working at age 65. Today only 31% of men aged 65 and only half of those aged 62 work. Among men aged 55, the proportion in the labor force dropped from over 90% in 1967 to 86% today.[4]

Americans are able to retire at increasingly younger ages because private pensions allow them to quit their jobs and still maintain a comfortable lifestyle. For workers who know how to use a calculator, it doesn't take much mathematical training to discover that early retirement is also a good investment. Early retirees get a bigger return on their pensions and Social Security than those who retire later.

Some experts argue that the early retirement trend will reverse by the time the baby boom reaches retirement age. Companies will change their pension policies to keep the leisure-loving baby boomers from draining pension funds and burdening the smaller working-age population that follows them. But with continued automation and immigration, businesses may be able to let the baby boom go. By 2020, most baby boomers will be retired.

Just as the middle-aged baby boomers will split into two economic camps—the affluent dual-income couples and the often struggling single-parent or single-earner families—old age will also divide the generation. On the up side will be the baby boomers who believed that some day they would be old; they planned ahead and saved for retirement. They will retire early and enjoy years of active leisure. On the down side will be the boomers who never discarded the live-for-today philosophy of youth. They will have to work long into their 60s and 70s. When the infirmities of age finally prevent them from working, they will depend on meager government handouts for support.

The baby boomers who will be affluent in old age may not be the same ones who will be affluent in middle age. The well off elderly will be those who had faith in the life expectancy tables, who knew that they would not be young forever.

WHAT IT'S LIKE TO BE OLD

Between 2011 and 2029, the entire baby-boom generation will turn 65. The consequences will be enormous. Census Bureau projections show that more than one in five Americans will be elderly by 2030, up from one in eight today.[5] Nobody knows what effect an enormous older generation will have on this country's politics, economics, and culture.

To younger people, the ages beyond 65 seem alike— gray hairs, failing health, grandchildren. But 85 is as different from 65 as 35 is from 15. We know more about what it's like to be 15 or 35 than we do 85, however, because in the past few people lived to be 85 to tell us. Now the story is starting to unfold, since the very old are one of the fastest growing age groups in the United States today.

There are three stages of old age. In each stage, the old live a different lifestyle.[6] First there is the go-go stage—the ages between 65 and 74. This is an active time, when people have the most independence and can fully enjoy their leisure. Many people in the go-go stage head South in the winter, take up long-abandoned hobbies, discover new interests, and travel.

The second stage of old age is the slow-go—from ages 75 to 84. People slow down, but they can still carry on most of their usual activities. Some slow-goers need help doing daily chores, but most continue to live independently.

The third and final stage is the no-go—ages 85 and up. Many people aged 85 and older need help with daily chores, and some also need skilled nursing services.

Americans are in the habit of ignoring the elderly because of attitudes that are rooted in the characteristics of the old in the 1950s, says William Lazer, professor of business administration at Florida Atlantic University.[7] Thirty years ago, there were relatively few elderly people in the population. Old age was a time of poor health and poverty. The elderly of the 1950s did not have the generous Social Security income and pensions upon which today's elderly depend.

All that changed. Today's elderly are like far younger people of past generations in their income, their health, their attitudes, and their activities. The number of Americans aged 65 and older increased from 12 million in 1950 to 30 million in 1987. The proportion of Americans who are aged 65 and older grew from 8% in 1950 to 12% today. In 2030, when the entire baby-boom generation is aged 65 or older, fully 21% of Americans will be elderly.

"Twenty years ago, only a slightly eccentric 55 year old woman would have been caught in public in a pair of blue jeans," says the advertising agency Jordan, Case & McGrath, Inc. "Just as the older segment was slow to accept changes in style, so too it remained separate from all other areas in the mainstream of society."[8] Today, however, the old follow in the footsteps of the young. They do not live for their children or grandchildren, but for themselves.

The attitudes of today's elderly are different in part because they are better educated than the elderly of the past. Forty-six percent of today's elderly are high school graduates, up from 18% in 1950.[9] As mentioned earlier, education is linked to a more active lifestyle. When the baby boom reaches its golden years, nearly 90% of the elderly will be high school graduates and 25% will have a college diploma. "Educated, mature consumers will be involved in more cultural activities—the arts, painting, books, symphonic music, and operas. They will seek a more graceful and elegant lifestyle," predicts Lazer.[10]

Money also is behind the changing attitudes of the elderly. Though people link old age with poverty, the two no longer go together because of the rise of private pensions and the indexing of Social Security benefits to inflation. In fact, families with no earners (the retired) are the only type of family whose incomes grew in the first half of the 1980s, after adjusting for inflation. The incomes of households headed by people aged 65 and older rose fully 16% between 1980 and 1985, while the incomes of households headed by younger people fell.[11]

Once they pay taxes, today's elderly have more money to spend per household member than do households headed by people younger than age 50. And the 27% of elderly households that have discretionary income have more of it than any other age group—$10,500 per household.[12]

In the next decade, the parents of the baby boom will retire. They will boost the incomes of the elderly even higher because they are retiring with more money than any previous older generation of Americans.

The parents of the baby boom are part of the small generation born between 1920 and 1935, when fertility in the United States fell and immigration slowed. This generation lived through the Depression and World War II, but it made more money than it expected to make on the job and in its investments in its homes. Three out of four families headed by this generation own homes today. Because of the rapid rise in housing prices during the 1970s, the homes owned by the parents of the baby boom are worth many times more than what they cost. Most homeowners aged 55 to 64 own their homes outright, and their home equity amounted to a median of

$54,000 in 1984, according to the Census Bureau.[13] The baby boom's parents spent most of their work life building Social Security and private pension benefits. More than 90% of them are covered by Social Security and two out of three also have employer- or union-provided pensions. The baby boom's parents will live comfortably on these benefits in their retirement years.

THE BABY BOOM'S FATE

The baby boom is not likely to live as well as its parents in old age. In fact, the baby boom may be headed for a disastrous retirement, according to Americans for Generational Equity (AGE), a nonpartisan organization whose goal is to increase public support for policies that will serve the economic interests of future generations. The baby boomers will have a longer retirement than any generation in history, according to Phillip Longman, the research director of AGE, but they cannot receive the benefits that today's elderly receive without placing too much of a burden on their children and grandchildren.[14] The low fertility of the baby-boom generation means there will be fewer than two workers to support each retiree by the year 2035.

Today, a person who retires at age 65 receives two types of benefits under the Social Security system: a monthly check from the Social Security trust fund and subsidized medical care through Medicare. Both benefits could be in trouble when the baby boom retires.

For the next few decades, the nation will have a huge work force (the baby boom) paying into the Social

Security trust fund and a relatively small generation (the baby boom's parents) drawing from the fund. When the baby boom retires, however, the scales will tip the other way. The large generation will draw more out of the fund than the smaller generation of workers can replace. The surplus should start to shrink in 2020.[15] Under the most optimistic forecast, the surplus will last until 2049. It all depends on how many children and grandchildren the baby boom has, and how long the baby boomers live.

Social Security will provide the baby boomers with some retirement income, but not as much as their parents will get. "Consider Social Security a nondeductible tax and look on any retirement benefit as a bonus," advises *Forbes* magazine.[16]

In order to support the aged baby boomers without impoverishing the nation's workers in the next century, the Social Security system will change. These changes could include raising the age at which the baby boom becomes eligible for full retirement benefits to 72, scaling back cost-of-living adjustments, or taxing or even eliminating the benefits that go to the high-income elderly.

There's more bad news: the elderly baby boomers will have to pay a much larger share of their health care costs than today's elderly because the Medicare system is in worse shape than the Social Security trust fund. Health care costs already absorb 10% of the annual expenditures of people aged 65 and older.[17] In their old age, the baby boomers will have to budget much more than that for prescription medicines, doctor bills, and hospital costs.

PLANNING AHEAD

The baby boom's retirement will be a long one. Those who retire at age 65 can expect to spend about 20 years of life in leisure pursuits.

If the length of retirement was set by law so that every generation had the same number of years of retirement as those who retired at age 65 in 1940, the baby boom could not retire until age 72 because life expectancy has increased so much. A man who retired in 1940 at age 65 could expect to spend 12 years in retirement before death.[18] Today, a 72-year-old man can expect about 12 more years of life.

The American economy cannot afford to support, in style, 20 years of retirement for one-fifth of its members. It is up to the baby boom to create the style in its old age. Some baby boomers will manage to do it because they will spend their work life building Social Security and pension benefits. Most married couples—because they have two incomes—will have at least one pension in retirement.

Many baby boomers worry about the solvency of Social Security. Only 35% of people younger than age 30 believe that Social Security will be there when they retire.[19] Among people aged 31 to 44, only 45% believe it will be there, according to an ABC News/Washington Post Poll. Just one out of five baby boomers think that Social Security will be their main source of retirement income. Instead, 70% say that personal investments, IRAs, or private pensions will be their main sources of income. Yet few baby boomers save for the rainy days of old age.

In a survey of professional baby boomers (those with the most money), *The Wall Street Journal* found that three out of four respondents were not planning adequately for retirement. "Unlike their parents, many of whom have vivid memories of Depression hardship, most of these young professionals have never known real need. So while many parents scraped and saved all their lives, their children never learned the habit of putting money aside for hard times," says *The Wall Street Journal*.[20]

SOCIAL SECURITY

Social Security is the major source of income for most of today's retirees. Despite the baby boomers' skepticism about Social Security, it will be the major source of income for many of them as well. The scheduled increases in Social Security taxes and the raising of the retirement age to 67 mean that Social Security benefits should be available for baby boomers into the middle of the next century. Social Security will account for 41% of the baby boom's retirement income on average, down from a 68% share among those retiring today, predicts Deborah Chollet of the Employee Benefit Research Institute.[21]

Using the EBRI pension and retirement income simulation model, Chollet predicts that at age 67 baby-boom couples will receive an average of $12,800 a year from Social Security (in 1985 dollars). Single baby boomers will receive an average of $6800 a year.[22] This may not sound like much, but it's better than what most baby boomers expect from Social Security.

PRIVATE PENSIONS

Most baby boomers can count on some kind of pension income in their retirement. The majority of baby boomers who work full time are covered by a pension, though many are not vested in a pension yet, according to the Employee Benefit Research Institute. Among two-earner couples, 49% of wives and 57% of husbands were covered by a private pension in 1983.[23] In total, two-thirds of two-earner couples have private pension coverage.

But many baby boomers who work part time or who change jobs frequently aren't building any pension benefits. And many pensions don't pay much. Among people retiring in 1984 after 30 years of service, those who earned $15,000 in the year before their retirement received a pension averaging only about $400 a month; those who earned $40,000 before their retirement received $900 a month, on average.[24] The baby boomers should get at least this much in pensions, but only if they demand it from their employers. The EBRI model predicts that pensions will supply the baby boomers with 32% of their retirement income.[25]

The tax reform plan enacted by Congress in 1986 will help the baby boom in its pursuit of pensions. Employers that provide pensions for their employees must now guarantee them a pension after only five years of employment instead of ten. For people who drift from job to job, and for women who drop out of the labor force to have children, this means many more will be covered by a pension in old age, though the pension may not pay much. At age 67, baby-boom couples who do have pen-

sions can expect to receive an average of $13,000 a year
(in 1985 dollars) in pension benefits.[26] Single boomers
who have pensions can expect to receive an average of
$9000.

THE IRA

Employer-provided pensions are the most common
retirement income program apart from Social Security.
IRAs also will add to retirement income, but now that
many people cannot deduct their IRA contributions from
taxable income, IRAs are not expected to provide much.

Until 1987, most workers could invest $2000 a year
in an IRA and deduct that amount from their taxable income. IRAs provided a nice tax deduction, but only
workers who could afford the $2000 sacrifice could take
advantage of it. That's why IRAs were more popular
among high-income workers than those with low incomes. Now, however, the IRA deduction is allowed
only for low- and moderate-income workers, those who
will need the IRAs the most in their old age since they
are less likely to have a pension and will receive less
from Social Security.

The EBRI predicts that while 41% of baby-boom families will have an IRA when they retire, it will provide
only 5% of retirement income.[27] Baby-boom couples
with IRAs will receive an average of $3000 a year (in 1985
dollars) from them, according to the EBRI, while the singles will receive an average of $2000 a year.

ADDING IT UP

The key to a comfortable old age is faith in the future. Married couples with checks coming from Social Security, pensions, and IRAs can expect a retirement income close to $30,000 a year on average, after adjusting for inflation. Many of these couples will have additional income from investments as well. They will be the affluent elderly, able to live where they want, travel when they want, and lend a helping hand to their children and grandchildren.

The unmarried baby boomers with Social Security, pensions, and IRAs can expect an income of about $18,000 a year after adjusting for inflation. This is enough for a comfortable lifestyle, including some travel.

But baby boomers who do not have pensions or savings will have to manage on much less money, possibly as little as $600 or $700 a month (in 1985 dollars). And then only if they've worked all their lives.

HOW THE OLD LIVE

In 1900, over half of the elderly lived with their children. Today, most older people live independently. The elderly live alone because they can afford it, and because they want to.

"Surveys of residential preference indicate that most elderly who live alone prefer to maintain their independence so long as their health and financial circumstances permit," say University of Michigan demographers Arland Thornton and Deborah Freedman.[28] The elderly are not pushed out of their children's homes—they decide against living with their children of their own free will. Today, 90% of men and women aged 65 and older are heading their own households.[29]

"With no models to guide them, the independent elderly are making new choices about how they want to live during a prolonged retirement," says Martha Farnsworth Riche, the editor of *The Numbers News*.[30] According to Riche, the retirement housing market began to take shape in the 1950s, when developers built communities—usually in the Sunbelt—just for retired people. Eight of the ten cities in the country with the largest proportion of elderly residents are in Florida, including Miami Beach, Clearwater, and St. Petersburg.[31] Over one-fifth of their populations are aged 65 or older. The sunbelt villages attract elderly married couples by offering them leisure activities, such as bridge tournaments and shopping trips, and providing them with services, such as house cleaning and lawn maintenance. Other retirement communities offer residents a variety of living arrangements. Residents choose whether to live in independent apartments, assisted-living apartments, or a nursing home, depending on their needs. As they age, the residents move from the independent apartments to the assisted-living apartments to the nursing home, if necessary.

Yet despite the increasing numbers of lifestyle options, few of the nation's elderly move when they retire because most older people prefer to stay right where they are. The 1980 census found that only 4% of people aged 65 or older lived in a different state in 1980 than in 1975, compared with 8% of all Americans.[32] Developers now are siting retirement communities throughout the country, so that the old can stay in their communities, yet take advantage of the activities and services of a self-contained retirement village.

By the time the baby boom retires it will be able to pick and choose the lifestyle it wants, from retirement villages in the Sunbelt to hotel-like living quarters in its hometowns. American businesses are already preparing for the day when one-fifth of Americans will be retired. Marriott Corporation, for example, is siting hotel-like communities for the elderly in metropolitan areas around the country.[33] For a fixed fee and monthly payments, these communities will provide residents with food, shelter, medical care, and other services for life. Marriott's target customers are elderly homeowners with incomes of at least $20,000 a year.

WHAT THE OLD DO

After being homebodies for decades, many baby boomers will leave home again in old age to explore the world. Today's older Americans are avid travelers—per capita spending on vacations is highest among people aged 55 and older.[34] And the affluent, elderly baby boomers—many of whom grew up hitching across the United States and Europe—will regard a trip to the Caribbean or to Europe as a weekend in the country.

The elderly baby-boom travelers will want exotic but comfortable vacations. Today's older travelers are exploring China, Iceland, Alaska, and other out-of-the-way places. The baby boom will want to explore and experience even more. This could create a new occupation—the "experience broker" who specializes in matching the experiences people want with the companies that can deliver them.

Exotic vacation packages accounted for only 5% of all vacation travel in 1985, according to *The Wall Street Journal*.[35] But as more companies offer more adventures, the exotic vacation will account for a growing share of travel: join a scientific expedition, conduct a symphony orchestra, live with a poor family, travel to the North Pole, solve a murder mystery, join in an African safari, star in a video movie.

"Education and prosperity are moving us to an experiential society, which we see in the explosive growth in such sports as sailing and hang gliding," says futurist Joseph F. Coates.[36] He predicts that vacations of the future will take tourists behind the scenes—to factories and back rooms of businesses in New Orleans, for example, or on an architectural tour of Chicago or an ethnic tour of New York City. How about a vacation during which the "tourist" builds an 18th century house, or lives in one for a few weeks?

Elderly travelers will use their vacations to increase their educations. "An increasingly prosperous and informed portion of the population wants to know more, not less, wants to see the real stuff, not the simulation, wants the full story, not the once-over-lightly gloss," says Coates.[37] That prosperous and informed portion of the population is the baby boom.

As people age, they vote more, volunteer more, and settle into community life. The aging of the baby boom will spur community renewal across the United States, resulting in a return of social conscience.

The baby boom will be a powerful political force in its old age. The college educated and the old are more likely to vote than other Americans. The baby boom will be both, and it will control politicians and policies from the golf courses, retirement villages, and European spas that it will populate. The dominance of the elderly baby boomers will not transform the United States into a stuffy and conservative land of the old, however. Instead, the baby boom's old age will bring an end to the conservative, middle-aged society of the next few decades. As noted earlier, people aged 60 and older are, in general, less conservative than people in their 40s and 50s.

A society dominated by the old will be less concerned with bread and butter issues. Most of the baby boomers will have paid off their mortgages; their work life will be over, their incomes secure, their children grown and on their own. A new social agenda will replace pocketbook issues, say Arthur Levine, President of Brandford College, and Jack Lindquist, president of Goddard College, in *The New York Times*.[38] Levine and Lindquist predict that progressive political candidates will be elected to office. Improving the cities and helping the poor will once again be high on the nation's list of priorities.

It will be the 1960s all over again, but it won't happen until about 2010. And unlike the social change of the 1960s—which was driven by teenagers who felt immortal—the social conscience of the 2010s will be tempered by the vulnerabilities of a generation that is getting to know death.

THE SEARCH FOR MEANING

Each year carries the baby boom closer to death. This fact of life will take its psychological toll as death claims increasing numbers of the friends and relatives of baby boomers in the next century. Death's approach will drive many baby boomers to search for the meaning of life, a search that will take many different forms.

As the baby boomers try to understand the meaning of life, they will explore death from many angles. Just as the nation searched for identity in the 1970s when the baby boomers were young adults, and as it searched for careers in the 1980s after the boomers discovered work, the nation will turn its attention to the baby boom's search for meaning in the 2030s. Death will top the bestseller list and claim the first-run movies on cable TV. It will be explored by psychologists in one-on-one counseling with baby boomers. Far Eastern philosophies, as in the 1960s, may once again grip the American imagination. Death will be the subject of entire courses in community colleges. Death may even be a college major, as baby boomers ask younger generations to hold their hands as they try to face the fact that it's now their turn.

The baby boom's grapple with death may lead some into despair. Most, however, will accept the inevitable.

CHAPTER 8

WHAT THE BABY BOOM WILL DIE OF

The oldest baby boomers, born in 1946, have 36 years of life left, on average. The youngest can expect to live for 53 more years.[1] But many baby boomers will live longer than the averages. Advances in medical technology should add at least a few more years to life by the time the baby boom reaches old age.

Today a person aged 65 can expect to live for 17 more years—or until age 82. In 1900, a 65-year-old only had about 12 years of life left. When actuaries calculate life expectancies, they assume that the chances of dying at each age will remain constant in the future. If no progress is made against heart disease, cancer, or other causes of death, then the actuarial tables are reasonable approximations of length of life. But medical science is making progress against some diseases.

A newborn girl today can expect to live to age 78 and a boy to age 71. But if we continue to make advances against disease in the next few decades as we did in the 1970s, then a newborn girl's life expectancy will actually be 90 years, and the boy's will be 81, say researchers John M. Owen and James W. Vaupel.[2]

Most people don't feel death approaching day to day. On a scale of one to ten, with one being terrible and ten being wonderful, most people feel pretty good no matter how old they are. People aged 65 and older rate their daily health at seven out of ten, according to Lois M. Verbrugge, a scientist at the University of Michigan's Institute of Gerontology.[3]

Sixty-nine percent of elderly men report that their health is excellent or good, compared with 79% of middle-aged men and 93% of young men. Seventy percent of elderly women report that their health is excellent or good, compared with 78% of middle-aged women and 90% of young women.

THE STAGES OF HEALTH

Verbrugge divides adult life into three stages of health: 18 to 44, 45 to 64, and 65 and older. Today the baby boom is moving from the young adult stage to the middle-age stage. It can expect many more aches and pains.

"Most of the daily discomforts of our lives are known only to ourselves and our families. There is no count of them in our national health statistics, which record only the problems that send us to a doctor, put us in the hospital, or kill us," says Verbrugge.[4]

In an attempt to track people's daily aches and pains, researchers asked a sample of Detroit residents to keep a six-week diary of their health, recording the days that they felt under the weather. Men aged 18 to 44 reported feeling symptoms on 13 of the 42 days in the study; the women reported symptoms on 18 days. "The single most common daily complaint of young adults was a headache," says Verbrugge.[5] But the common cold accounts for the greatest share of daily symptoms. Ranking second are muscular aches and pains. Feeling tired ranks third.

Young adults often drink and eat too much, sleep too little, and work too hard. They bring on themselves many of their daily health problems. Only a small proportion of young adults have chronic health conditions—defined as an illness that lingers for three or more months. Among those who have chronic conditions, allergies are the most common, followed by back problems.

By middle age, the health problems of daily life change. But the number of days people feel under the weather does not change much. The middle-aged men in the Detroit study reported symptoms of illness on 11 days of the 42-day study, while middle-aged women reported symptoms on 19 days.

Aches and pains are the biggest problems for the middle-aged, while colds and flu fall to second place. The body stiffens as it ages, and arthritis becomes an important problem. "In contrast to young adults, diseases are now the main causes of daily health problems," says Verbrugge.[6]

Even among the elderly, the good days outnumber the bad. The elderly in the Detroit study reported 18 days of symptoms during the 42-day study. Aches and pains are by far the most common daily complaint of the old. Among men the aches are in the legs, hands, back, feet, shoulders, knees, and hips. Among women the pains are in the knees, legs, back and shoulders. Colds are much less troublesome in old age. But chronic conditions become important—arthritis, hypertensive disease, heart conditions, and hearing impairments. While the baby boomers' concern with fitness and nutrition may delay the onset of some of these conditions, the generation cannot escape them.

Throughout life, women report more daily health problems than men, Verbrugge reports, but men are more likely to have fatal chronic diseases. "Women tend to be sicker than men in the short run," she says, "while men are sicker than women in the long run."[7]

All told, people are sick in bed an average of about three days a year. The number of days people are sick in bed does not vary much by age, but what keeps people in bed does.[8]

Every year, about one-third of Americans get a cold. Three out of four young children get a cold each year. This proportion drops dramatically as people get older.[9] Twenty-seven percent of people aged 25 to 44 catch a cold each year, 20% of 45- to 64-year-olds, and just 14% of the elderly. It seems that aging has its trade-offs: people escape the running nose and sore throat, but they are more likely to develop a problem that they can't shake.

Most of the health problems on the baby boom's current list of chronic complaints are not serious. First comes sinus problems, suffered by 14%.[10] Hay fever strikes 11%. Back trouble plagues 7%; high blood pressure, 6% (the only life-threatening condition on the list); arthritis, 6%; and hemorrhoids, 5%. Another 3% of the baby boomers still face that teenage scourge, acne.

The baby boom's list of chronic problems will get more serious as it ages. After arthritis, the most common chronic problem for people aged 45 to 64 is high blood pressure, affecting 25%. Hearing problems affect 14% of today's 45- to 64-year-olds. But a much larger proportion of baby boomers will suffer from hearing problems in middle and old age because loud music has already done permanent damage to their ears.

Among the elderly, arthritis and high blood pressure are the most common chronic problems. Fifty percent have arthritis, while high blood pressure affects 39%. Third is heart disease, and fourth is hearing problems, affecting 30%. Ten percent of the elderly have trouble seeing, and 15% have cataracts.

These are going to be the baby boom's problems in old age as well, with arthritis and hearing problems ranking first and second. Medical science has made no progress against arthritis, so half of the baby boom can expect to suffer from its aches and pains in old age. And as they age, one-third of baby boomers will find the world's sounds growing faint.

But the baby boom might be less likely to suffer from heart disease than today's elderly. The baby boomers are eating less red meat, fewer eggs, and more green vegetables than their grandparents. They are getting more exercise, and the men are less likely to smoke. A decline in deaths due to heart disease has already contributed to a longer life for the old. The baby boomers' healthy habits could lengthen their lives even more.

CARING FOR THE ELDERLY

Through Social Security, the federal government provides financial support for the nation's elderly. Because of this, it's uncommon—and usually unnecessary—for Americans to support their elderly relatives financially. This fact has created a popular myth: that elderly parents can't count on their children to take care of them. In fact, they can. A large proportion of middle-aged Americans spend much of their time helping their elderly relatives. A survey by the Traveler's Corporation shows, for example, that one-fifth of its employees older than age 30 care for an elderly relative.[11] On average, these employees spend 10 hours a week helping their relatives.

Even in a modern, wealthy society, and despite the enormous Social Security system, the elderly need children as insurance for a happy and healthy old age. The millions of baby boomers who consider remaining childless do not realize that the most important long-term investment they can make is to have children. It's not the childless who are selfish. It's the people who have children who are selfishly—and wisely—guarding their old age.

Few of the young elderly need much help, but a large share of those aged 85 and older need assistance. Only 6% of people aged 65 to 74 and 14% of those aged 75 to 84 need help with daily tasks. But among those aged 85 and older, fully 40% need help.[12] Shopping is the most difficult activity for the very old to do on their own, followed by household chores, cooking, cleaning, and handling money. Families provide fully 80% to 90% of the personal care, household maintenance, transportation, and shopping services for their elderly relatives, says the Population Reference Bureau.[13]

In addition, children provide their elderly parents with social support. "Most elderly parents live near at least one child," reports the Population Reference Bureau.[14]

In a study of elderly people who live alone, the National Center for Health Statistics finds that among those with children, 72% live within minutes of at least one child. Twenty-three percent of the elderly who live alone see one of their children every day. An additional 40% see a child at least weekly.[15]

Today, the telephone has replaced the mail as the way for families to keep in touch. Forty-three percent of the elderly who live alone never get a letter from their children, but 36% talk to their children on the telephone every day. Another 41% talk to their children on the phone at least once a week.[16]

Because Americans are living longer, the extended family is more real today than in the past. Families now typically include three or four generations, while families earlier in this century had only two or three, according to the Census Bureau.

"By the year 2000, the typical family is expected to be a four-generation family," says the bureau in its analysis of aging.[17] But because so many baby boomers will be childless, their link with the extended family will be through brothers, sisters, nieces, and nephews instead of sons and daughters. The burden of caring for the aged baby boomers could fall heavily on those nieces and nephews, who may shun the task because they will have their own parents to care for.

The Census Bureau predicts that by the time the baby boomers are old, there will be a shortage of family members who can provide the boomers with the support they will need. The Census Bureau can foresee this problem by comparing the number of old people in the population with the number of middle-aged.[18] This ratio will be favorable in 2005, at 114 old people for every 100 middle-aged. The elderly of 2005 (the baby boom's parents) will be well taken care of (by the many baby boomers).

But by the year 2025—when the baby boomers born in 1960 turn 65—the ratio of the old to the middle-aged will be 253 to 100. There will more than twice as many elderly baby boomers as middle-aged adults to look after them.

Many of the baby boom's children will face double duty in their middle age—looking after their elderly parents and their own children at the same time. "Many persons aged 45 to 49 will have the joint tasks of supporting both an aged parent or parents, often over 70 years of age, and children of college age," says the Census Bureau.[19]

As the baby boomers age into their 80s, many will be dependent on children who are themselves elderly. "The possible financial and psychic burden on the individual families may be tremendous if there are two generations of elderly people," says the Census Bureau.[20]

Traditionally, the middle-aged housewife is the family caretaker. But housewives are becoming increasingly rare. This means that working baby-boom men and women will have to find the free time to help out their parents in the next few decades. When the baby boom itself is old, its hard-working children are likely to be just as busy as the baby boom is today. They too probably will find the time to help their elderly parents because the strength of family ties endures.

But what about the childless? When the brittle bones of old age limit their independence, the childless baby boomers will have to band together, live communally, and pool their resources. Because there will be so many of them, businesses will find it profitable to solve their problems. One solution may be to bring back the commune.

Only 40,000 Americans live in communes today.[21] The commune peaked in popularity in the 1960s when many baby boomers tried it, but few made communal life work. Communes might succeed in the next century, however, as the millions of childless baby boomers rally together for friendship and support.

NURSING HOMES

Few elderly people live in nursing homes because, for most families, institutionalization is a last resort. A large proportion of the institutionalized elderly, in fact, are in institutions because they have no children, according to the Population Reference Bureau.[22]

In the next few decades, some baby boomers will face the painful decision of whether to put their parents in a nursing home. For one out of four baby boomers who live to the age of 65, someone will have to make that decision for them someday.[23]

Less than 2% of people aged 65 to 74 are in nursing homes. Among people aged 75 to 84, only 7% are institutionalized. But 22% of people aged 85 and older are in nursing homes—still a minority, but a sizeable one.[24]

An estimated 6.6 million Americans aged 65 and older need long-term care today, according to the Employee Benefit Research Institute (EBRI).[25] EBRI projects that by 2000, 9.3 million elderly will need long-term care, and by 2040 (when the baby boom is aged 76 to 94), fully 19 million elderly will require long-term care.

Yet medical insurance rarely covers such a catastrophe, and nursing home expenses average $25,000 a year. "Nearly two-thirds of the persons who enter nursing homes become impoverished in just over three months," says EBRI.[26]

The parents of the baby boom face this insurance problem today when they are forced to put their disabled, aged parents into nursing homes. They watch their parents' assets, built up over a lifetime, disappear in a matter of months. But insurance companies realize that there might be a market in covering long-term care. The incomes of the elderly are rising, and more can afford the cost of nursing home insurance. EBRI estimates that such insurance would cost between $800 and $1300 a year depending on how old people are when they take out a policy.[27]

Most elderly Americans mistakenly believe that they have nursing home insurance. "How do you sell it to people who think they've already got it?" asks Paul Wiligang, deputy executive vice president of the American Health Care Association.[28] In fact, neither Medicare nor most private health insurance policies cover long-term care. But the awareness of the need for such insurance among today's elderly is growing as they see their disabled friends become destitute because of nursing home costs. By the time the baby boomers face their own long-term care costs, nursing home insurance could be as commonplace as auto insurance. Its expense will add to the steep health care costs for which the elderly baby boomers will have to budget.

By the time the baby boom is very old, however, institutionalization may be less common than it is today. "Home maintenance problems are the key reason people leave their homes. It becomes increasingly difficult for them to live independently," says Katie Sloan of the American Association of Retired Persons.[29] About 30% of nursing home residents are there because they don't have housing options, says Sloan. Meals on wheels, home chore services, and home health care are cost-effective ways to care for people outside of a nursing home. Over half of Americans want to see expanded adult day care and home health care services in their

communities, according to a survey by the National
Research Corporation, a health care research company.[30] Community outreach services such as these may
be the only way that the nation can afford the baby
boom's old age.

THE RISE OF WOMEN

Americans have a 95% chance of living to their 40th
birthdays. Few people die before they reach middle age.
But from then on, the odds get worse.

Three out of four baby boomers will celebrate their
65th birthdays. Nearly half will make it to their 80th
birthdays. One in three will live to the age of 85.[31]

Because women live longer than men, women's
chances of living to ripe old age are much greater than
men's. Only 21% of baby-boom men will live to age 85,
but 41% of baby-boom women will live that long. These
skewed statistics mean that as the baby boom ages, it is
becoming increasingly female.

When the baby boomers were children, boys outnumbered girls because for every 100 girl babies born,
105 boy babies are born. Boys need that kind of head
start because they soon fall behind. Already, there are
slightly more women baby boomers than men. This gap
will widen rapidly as the generation heads into old age,
because at every age men are more likely to die than
women. By the time the peak of the baby boom (people
born in 1957) hits age 85, there will be only 60 baby-
boom men left for every 100 baby-boom women.[32]

At birth, the gap in the life expectancy between boys and girls is seven years. The gap shrinks slightly as people age, but even at age 85, women's life expectancy is nearly two years longer than that for men.[33] If a baby-boom husband and wife are the same age, the chances are better than 50–50 that the wife will outlive her husband.

Seven out of ten baby-boom women will outlive their husbands. Only three out of ten baby-boom husbands will outlive their wives.[34] A baby-boom woman can expect to become a widow at age 68 and spend an average of 15 years alone, according to demographers Jacob S. Siegel and Cynthia M. Teauber.[35]

No one knows precisely why women live longer than men, but both biological predispositions (women's genes and hormones protect them from cardiovascular disease) and social factors (women are less likely than men to die in accidents) contribute to the statistics. As women's lives become more like men's, their statistical advantage may disappear. "Throughout this century," says gerontologist Lois M. Verbrugge, "American females have had a sizable longevity advantage over males. Around 1920 that advantage began to increase sharply, and each decade thereafter showed a widening gender gap."[36] Now there are signs of a reversal, notes Verbrugge. The gap in life expectancy between men and women has closed slightly as mortality rates for some diseases decline more rapidly for men than for women.

Verbrugge sees a possibility of a further narrowing of the life expectancy gap as men's and women's roles become more alike. This should lead to more similarity in men's and women's death rates as well. But these changes won't occur fast enough to make a difference for the baby-boom generation. Already, most baby boomers are women. In old age the numerical gap will be much greater. The women of the baby boom should ponder their unisex future every now and then, making sure to forge friendships with other women that will last a long lifetime.

WHAT WILL KILL THE BABY BOOM?

Infectious diseases once killed most Americans. Today, such diseases kill fewer than one in ten of us. Among 100 people aged 65 and older, on average 44 will die of heart disease, 22 of cancer, and 12 of stroke.[37] In 1900, the median age at death was 36—half of Americans died before their 36th birthday and half after. By 1980, the median age of death was 72.

Americans have conquered many of the diseases of infancy and youth. For the baby boom, the diseases of old age lie ahead.

Even if scientists found a cure for cancer and eliminated heart disease, the baby boom would not live forever. A cancer cure would increase life expectancy for people aged 65 by only two years. Ending heart disease would increase it by only seven years. Eliminating one cause of death only makes other causes of death more important.

Of course it's unlikely that either heart disease or cancer will be completely eliminated in the next few decades. While scientists may make some progress against fatal diseases, the major killers of Americans are likely to be the baby boom's killers as well.

In the year 2046, the first baby boomer will turn 100. The last will turn 100 in 2064. Today, the chances of living to age 100 are better than ever.

Already, the number of people aged 100 and older is growing rapidly without any help from the baby boom. There are now an estimated 41,000 people aged 100 and older in the United States out of a population of 243 million, according to the Census Bureau.[38] This number should increase to more than 100,000 by the turn of the century as medical science makes progress against the diseases of old age. When the baby boom hits 100, the number of centenarians will grow by more than 1 million in just 20 years, from 760,000 in 2045 to 1.7 million by 2065. By 2080, the Census Bureau projects that there could be 1.9 million Americans aged 100 or older out of a total population of 311 million.

Not even one baby boomer will be alive by 2080. The youngest would be 116 in that year, and few if any humans have ever lived that long. The baby-boom generation will cease to exist in about 2069—a few years after the return of Halley's Comet.

CHAPTER 9

CONCLUSION

The new rules of economic life drive America's future. The two-earner family is more important to predictions about what will happen to the baby boom than any other factor except the inevitable, inexorable aging of the generation. The two-earner family shapes the baby boom's work life, its home life, and even its psychological well-being.

The more money a wife makes relative to her husband, the more housework her husband does. As women take on the responsibilities of providing for their families, men shoulder more responsibilities at home. This is a fact of baby-boom life, yet both men and women feel guilty about it because they live differently than their parents. Men wonder why they don't earn as much money as their fathers; women wonder why their husbands can't support them like their fathers supported their mothers. Men wonder why their wives don't keep house like their mothers. Women wonder why they have such a hard time keeping up with the housework when their mothers made it look so easy.

Some baby boomers feel like failures. Few realize that the way they live is not a choice but an adaptation to a transformed American economy. The baby boomers enthusiastically adopted the new rules; now, some find they are the victims of the rules. Men and women want opportunity, but they also want simplicity. Unfortunately, only a few baby boomers will have both. The handful of baby-boom men who can command exorbitant salaries will be able to live the 1950s lifestyle. Their wives will work only if they want to. In contrast, most baby-boom women will have to work just as most baby-boom men must work.

Predictions about the baby boom must consider the fact that the values of the generation are nearly identical to the values of older generations of Americans. Baby boomers believe in marriage, home, family, and God. Because of this, the lives of middle-aged baby boomers—most of whom will be homeowning, married couples with children—will center on the family. And because the baby boom is one-third of Americans, the nation's attention also will focus on home and family.

Though their families are complex—because of the new rules of life—baby boomers still think love is the most important reason to marry. They still advocate a lifetime marriage to one person, and they still believe that the ideal family has at least two children.

Predictions about the future of the baby boom must account for the fact that this is the best-educated generation in history. Though it shares the values of older generations of Americans, the baby boom's educational level makes its lifestyle different. The educational level of the baby boom splintered the mass market. Education creates diversity, and the middle-aged consumers of the next few decades will be increasingly difficult to pigeonhole. The result will be more of everything—more technology in the home, more imported goods and exotic foods, more ways of buying things, and more things to buy. Consumers will demand choice, and successful businesses of the future will deliver it. The baby boom will dictate its wants and needs to business for the next five decades.

Some things are predictable because what people do at certain ages is predictable. In middle age, people spend money. Today, society condemns the baby boomers for spending too much and saving too little. But the generation is guilty only of needing too much—it needs houses, appliances, furniture, cars, work clothes, and so on. In a few decades the generation will have most of what it needs, and it will begin to save money. Then society will accuse the baby boom of being too tight with the purse strings.

The baby boom may battle advancing age, but its middle age will be the prime of its life. It's difficult to predict what the baby boom's old age will be like because the generation is deciding right now how it will turn out. The happiness of the baby boom in old age hinges on two things: children and money.

Unfortunately, most Americans believe the myth that parents cannot count on their children in old age. Because American society has been so slow to adjust to the new rules of economic life, it is doubly hard for the baby boom to make the best long-term investment that it can make—the investment in children. Not only is the baby boom terribly misled by the belief that children don't matter in old age, it is sabotaged by the lack of public policy that could make it easier to have children. The baby boom needs affordable day care and flexible work schedules.

Perhaps in middle age the baby boom will take aging more seriously. If so, it may get tough on its employers. Social Security will not support the boomers in the style to which they will become accustomed in their middle age. And it is beyond the means of most baby boomers to save enough of their earnings for a comfortable retirement. Instead, employer-provided pensions will make or break the generation in the final decades of its life.

In middle age, the huge size of the baby-boom generation will work in its favor. In old age, its huge size could crush it. The well-being of baby boomers in old age depends on their breaking away from the crowd and provisioning themselves for survival as their health fails. Those who stock up well with money and family will enjoy their leisure years. Those who don't will have to depend on the good will of a society that finds the baby boom a burden, and on the compassion of younger people who live in the baby boom's shadow. Most baby boomers are not used to being poor, but many may be poor in old age.

No one predicted the baby boom when it started as a fad in the frenzy of victory after World War II. But it is easy to predict the baby boom's end in the middle of the next century after disrupting American society for ten decades. The baby boom created new traditions of life that will last long after the generation disappears. The demographic ripples in the American pond will be visible for generations, spreading ever outward as the baby boom's children and grandchildren have children. Eventually, however, the ripples will fade and a new demographic disturbance, independent of the baby boom, will make its own waves. But for the next 50 years, the consequences of two firm lips and a slice of heaven, multiplied by the millions, will power American society.

NOTES

2. THE BOOM

1. Advertisement, *Life*, 2 June 1945, inside front cover.
2. Advertisement, *Life*, 13 August 1945, p. 1.
3. Advertisement, *Life*, 4 June 1945, inside front cover.
4. Ibid.
5. Personal telephone conversation with National Center for Health Statistics, 8 August 1985.
6. U.S. Bureau of the Census, *Historical Statistics of the United States, Colonial Times to 1970, Part 1* (Washington, D.C.: U.S. Government Printing Office, 1975), p. 49.

7. Joseph Veroff, Elizabeth Douvan, and Richard A. Kulka, *The Inner American—A Self Portrait from 1957 to 1976* (New York: Basic Books, Inc., 1981), p. 147.

8. Edward L. Kain, "Surprising Singles," *American Demographics*, August 1984, p. 19.

9. U.S. Bureau of the Census, *Historical Statistics*, p. 64.

10. Ibid., p. 49.

11. Leonard Gross, "America's Mood Today," *Look*, 29 June 1965, p. 21.

12. U.S. Bureau of the Census, "Projections of the Population of the United States, by Age, Sex, and Race: 1983 to 2080," *Current Population Reports*, Series P-25, No. 952, May 1984, Table 6.

13. U.S. Bureau of the Census, "Money Income of Households, Families, and Persons in the United States: 1984," *Current Population Reports*, Series P-60, No. 151, April 1986, Table 11.

14. Leon F. Bouvier, "America's Baby Boom Generation: The Fateful Bulge," *Population Bulletin*, Volume 35, No. 1 (Washington, D.C.: Population Reference Bureau, 1980), p. 5.

15. Richard A. Easterlin, *Birth and Fortune—The Impact of Numbers on Personal Welfare* (New York: Basic Books, Inc., 1980), p. ix.

16. Norman B. Ryder, "A Model of Fertility by Planning Status," *Demography*, Volume 15, No. 4, November 1978, p. 455.

17. William F. Pratt, William D. Mosher, Christine A. Bachrach, and Marjorie C. Horn, "Understanding U.S. Fertility: Findings from the National Survey of Family Growth, Cycle III," *Population Bulletin*, Volume 39, No. 5 (Washington, D.C.: Population Reference Bureau, 1984), p. 31.

18. Bouvier, p. 11.

19. Gross, p. 21.

20. "American Woman's Dilemma," *Life*, 16 June 1947, pp. 101–116.

21. Ibid., p. 110.

22. "Changing Roles of Modern Marriage," *Life*, 24 December 1956, p. 109.

23. Ibid., p. 116.

24. Betty Friedan, *The Feminine Mystique* (New York: Dell Publishing Company, Inc., 1963), p. 38.

25. Ibid., p. 44.

26. Barbara Ehrenreich, *The Hearts of Men—American Dreams and the Flight From Commitment* (New York: Anchor Books, 1983), p. 17.

27. Ibid., p. 18.

28. U.S. Bureau of the Census, "Money Income," Table 11.

29. Fabian Linden, "The American Way To Get Ahead," *American Demographics*, December 1986, p. 4.

30. Gross, p. 21.

31. U.S. Bureau of the Census, "Population Profile of the United States: 1982," *Current Population Reports*, Special Studies, Series P-23, No. 130, December 1983, p. 54.

32. Cheryl Russell and Thomas G. Exter, "America at Mid-Decade," *American Demographics*, January 1986, p. 29.

33. U.S. Bureau of the Census, "Education in the United States: 1940–1983," *Special Demographic Analysis*, CDS-85-1, 1985, p. 46.

34. U.S. Bureau of the Census, "Educational Attainment in the United States: March 1981 and 1980," *Current Population Reports*, Series P-20, No. 390, August 1984, p. 2.

35. U.S. Bureau of the Census, "Education," p. 5.

36. Russell and Exter, p. 29.

37. National Center for Education Statistics, *The Condition of Education, 1985 Edition* (Washington, D.C.: U.S. Government Printing Office, 1985), pp. 124, 128.

38. The Roper Organization, *Roper Reports 85-2* (New York: The Roper Organization, Inc., 1985).

39. American Council of Life Insurance and the Health Insurance Association of America, *The Baby Boom Generation* (Washington, D.C.: American Council of Life Insurance and the Health Insurance Association of America, 1983), pp. 25-31.

40. Bouvier, p. 12.

41. Frank Levy and Richard C. Michel, "Are Baby Boomers Selfish?," *American Demographics*, April 1985, p. 38.

42. U.S. Bureau of the Census, *Statistical Abstract of the United States: 1986*, 106th edition (Washington, D. C.: U.S. Government Printing Office, 1985), p. 737.

43. American Council on Education, *National Norms for Entering College Freshmen—Fall 1967*, ACE Research Reports, Volume 2, No. 7 (Washington, D.C.: American Council on Education, 1967), pp. 34-36.

44. American Council on Education and the University of California at Los Angeles, *The American Freshman: National Norms for Fall 1982* (University of California, Los Angeles: Cooperative Institutional Research Program of the University of California and the American Council on Education, 1982), pp. 56-57, 62.

45. National Center for Education Statistics, *High School Seniors: A Comparative Study of the Classes of 1972 and 1980*, NCES 84-202, High School and Beyond, A National Longitudinal Study for the 1980s (Washington, D.C.: U.S. Government Printing Office, 1984), pp. 11, 15.

46. Ibid., p. 25.

47. "American Values: Change and Stability—A Conversation with Daniel Yankelovich," *Public Opinion*, December/January 1984, pp. 2–8.

48. American Council on Education, *National Norms for Entering College Freshmen—Fall 1967*, pp. 34–36; American Council on Education and the University of California at Los Angeles, *The American Freshman: National Norms for Fall 1982*, pp. 56–57, 62.

49. The House & Garden Louis Harris Study, "How the Baby Boom Generation is Living Now" (New York: Conde Nast Publications, Inc., 1981), p. 7.

50. Thomas J. Lueck, "Baby-Boomers: Reality vs. Dream," *The New York Times*, 6 March 1986, pp. C1, C12.

51. Thomas F. Cash, Barbara A. Winstead, and Louis H. Janda, "The Great American Shape-Up," *Psychology Today*, April 1986, pp. 30–37.

52. National Center for Health Statistics, "Provisional Data from the Health Promotion and Disease Prevention Supplement to the National Health Interview Survey: United States, January–March 1985," *NCHS Advance Data*, No. 113, 15 November 1985, p. 3.

53. Patricia Morrisroe, "Forever Young," *New York*, 9 June 1986, p. 44.

54. Ibid.

55. "From 'Old' to 'New' to 'Classic'," *USA Today*, 11 July 1985, p. B-1.

56. Bill Backer cited in Scott Kilman, "Coca-Cola Co. To Bring Back Its Old Coke," *The Wall Street Journal*, 11 July 1985, p. 2.

57. Pamela G. Hollie, "Keeping New Coke Alive," *The New York Times*, 20 July 1986, p. F6.

3. THE NEW RULES

1. U.S. Bureau of the Census, "Money Income," Table 16.

2. U.S. Bureau of the Census, 1986 Current Population Survey, unpublished data.

3. Greg J. Duncan, *Years of Poverty, Years of Plenty: The Changing Economic Fortunes of American Workers and Families* (Ann Arbor: The University of Michigan Institute for Social Research, Survey Research Center, 1984), p. 28.

4. U.S. Bureau of the Census, "Earnings in 1983 of Married-Couple Families, by Characteristics of Husbands and Wives," *Current Population Reports*, Series P-60, No. 153, March 1986, Tables 1A, 1C.

5. United States League of Savings Institutions, *Homeownership/Returning to Tradition* (Chicago: United States League of Savings Institutions, 1986), p. 16.

6. U.S. Bureau of the Census, "Money Income," Table 16.

7. U.S. Bureau of the Census, "Money Income," Table 16.

8. This calculation is based on men's incomes in 1963 and 1984 in U.S. Bureau of the Census, "Money Income," Table 28; median cost of a new home in 1963 and 1984, published Census Bureau data; and median costs of real estate taxes, utilities, and insurance in United States League of Savings Institutions, p. 7.

9. George Sternlieb and James W. Hughes, "Running Faster to Stay in Place," *American Demographics*, June 1982, p. 19.

10. U.S. Bureau of the Census, "Household and Family Characteristics: March 1984," *Current Population Reports*, Series P-20, No. 398, April 1985, Table 3.

11. Bureau of Labor Statistics, *Labor Force Statistics Derived from the Current Population Survey*, Volume 1, Bulletin 2096, September 1982, pp. 716, 722.

12. Howard Hayghe, "Working Mothers Reach Record Number in 1984," Research Summaries, *Monthly Labor Review*, Bureau of Labor Statistics, December 1984, p. 31.

13. Ibid.

14. *The 1985 Virginia Slims American Women's Opinion Poll*, a Study Conducted by The Roper Organization, Inc. (New York, Virginia Slims, 1986), p. 87.

15. Howard N. Fullerton, Jr., "The 1995 Labor Force: BLS' Latest Projections," *Monthly Labor Review*, Bureau of Labor Statistics, November 1985, p. 22.

16. F. Thomas Juster, "Preferences for Work and Leisure," *Economic Outlook USA*, Survey Research Center, University of Michigan, Volume 13, No. 1, First Quarter 1986, pp. 15–17.

17. U.S. Bureau of the Census, "Money Income," Table 16.

18. Kingsley Davis, "Wives and Work: The Sex Role Revolution and Its Consequences, *Population and Development Review*, Volume 10, No. 3, September 1984, pp. 397–417.

19. Shirley J. Smith, "Revised Worklife Tables Reflect 1979–80 Experience," *Monthly Labor Review*, Bureau of Labor Statistics, August 1985, pp. 23–29.

20. U.S. Bureau of the Census, *Statistical Abstract of the United States: 1986*, p. 400.

21. Anne McDougall Young, "One-Fourth of the Adult Labor Force are College Graduates," Research Summaries, *Monthly Labor Review*, Bureau of Labor Statistics, February 1985, p. 43.

22. George T. Silvestri and John M. Lukasiewicz, "Occupational Employment Projections: The 1984–95 Outlook," *Monthly Labor Review*, Bureau of Labor Statistics, November 1985, pp. 42–57.

23. U.S. Bureau of the Census, 1984 Current Population Survey, unpublished data.

24. Robert E. Hall, "The Importance of Lifetime Jobs in the U.S. Economy," *American Economic Review*, September 1982, pp. 716–724, as cited in Employee Benefit Research Institute, "Pension Vesting Standards: ERISA and Beyond," *EBRI Issue Brief*, No. 51, February 1986, p. 8.

25. Employee Benefit Research Institute, "Pension Vesting Standards: ERISA and Beyond," *EBRI Issue Brief*, No. 51, February 1986, pp. 11, 12.

26. Ellen Sehgal, "Occupational Mobility and Job Tenure in 1983," *Monthly Labor Review*, October 1984, pp. 18–23.

27. The Roper Organization, Inc., *Roper Reports 85-2*, p. 238.

28. U.S. Bureau of the Census, 1986 Current Population Survey, unpublished data.

29. U.S. Bureau of the Census, "Education in the United States: 1940–1983," p. 11.

30. U.S. Bureau of the Census, "Money Income," Table 29.

31. U.S. Bureau of the Census, "Money Income and Poverty Status of Families and Persons in the United States: 1985 (Advance Data From the March 1986 Current Population Survey)," *Current Population Reports*, Series P-60, No. 154, August 1986, Table 10.

32. Ibid., Table 14.

33. Wharton Econometric Forecasting Associates income projections for households headed by 35- to 44-year-olds, cited in Demographic Forecasts, *American Demographics*, July 1986, p. 58.

34. U.S. Bureau of the Census, "Money Income (Advance Data)," Tables 18, 19.

35. Fabian Linden, "The Dream is Alive," *American Demographics*, June 1986, pp. 4, 6.

36. U.S. Bureau of the Census, "Money Income (Advance Data)," Tables 10, 14.

37. Ibid., Table 10.

38. Bureau of Labor Statistics, "Weekly Earnings of Wage and Salary Workers: Second Quarter, 1986," USDL 86-305, 1986.

39. U.S. Bureau of the Census, "Money Income," Table 33.

40. David E. Bloom, "Women and Work," *American Demographics*, September 1986, p. 27.

41. James P. Smith and Michael P. Ward, *Women's Wages and Work in the Twentieth Century* (Santa Monica, California: The Rand Corporation, Inc., 1984), p. xiv.

42. U.S. Bureau of the Census, "Earnings in 1983 of Married-Couple Families," p. 7.

43. Suzanne M. Bianchi, "Wives Who Earn More Than Their Husbands," *American Demographics*, July 1984, pp. 19–23, 44.

44. *Virginia Slims*, p. 83.

45. Stephen J. Rose, *The American Profile Poster—Who Owns What, Who Makes How Much, Who Works Where & Who Lives with Whom* (New York: Pantheon Books, 1986), pp. 9–11.

46. Ibid., p. 9.

47. David Landis, "Location Still Rules Over Price of Homes," *USA Today*, 4 August 1986, p. B-1.

48. Wharton, Demographic Forecasts, p. 58.

49. Courtenay Slater, "The Working Rich," *American Demographics*, July 1985, pp. 4, 6–7.

50. FIND/SVP, *The Affluent Market* (New York: FIND/SVP, The Information Clearing House, Inc., March 1984), p. 4.

51. Wharton, Demographic Forecasts, p. 58.

52. U.S. Bureau of the Census, "Money Income (Advance Data)," Table 14.

53. Wharton, Demographic Forecasts, p. 58.

54. Wharton Econometric Forecasting Associates income projections for households headed by 45- to 54-year-olds, cited in Demographic Forecasts, *American Demographics*, August 1986, p. 58.

55. U.S. Bureau of the Census, "Lifetime Earnings Estimates for Men and Women in the United States: 1979," *Current Population Reports*, Series P-60, No. 139, February 1983, p. 3.

56. David E. Bloom and Michael P. Martin, "Fringe Benefits à la Carte," *American Demographics*, February 1983, pp. 22–25, 49.

57. Judith Langer, "Langer Addresses ARF on Future Trends, Techniques," press release issued by Anita Hunter Associates, 12 May 1986.

58. Interview with Helen Axel, "Baby Boomers Rearranging Benefit Plans," *Syracuse Post Standard*, 9 September 1985, pp. D-1, D-6.

59. Dana E. Friedman, "Child Care for Employees' Kids," Special Report, *Harvard Business Review*, March–April 1986, pp. 28–34.

60. Bureau of Labor Statistics, *Employee Benefits in Medium and Large Firms, 1985*, Bulletin 2262, 1986.

61. *Virginia Slims*, p. 99.

62. Employee Benefit Research Institute analysis cited in Betsy Morris, "Frequent Job Changes May Hurt Young Workers Upon Retirement," *The Wall Street Journal*, 24 July 1986, Section 2, p. 1.

63. Employee Benefit Research Institute, "Pension Vesting Standards," pp. 1, 15.

64. Betsy Morris, "Frequent Job Changes May Hurt Young Workers Upon Retirement," *The Wall Street Journal*, 24 July 1986, Section 2, p. 1.

65. U.S. Bureau of the Census, "Money Income," Table 36.
66. Eugene H. Becker, "Self-Employed Workers: An Update to 1983," *Monthly Labor Review*, July 1984, pp. 14–18.

4. THE NEW HOMEMAKERS

1. John Bongaarts, "Building a Family: Unplanned Events," *Population Notes 52*, Center for Policy Studies, The Population Council, 29 December 1983, p. 10.
2. Toni Richards, Michael J. White, and Amy Ong Tsui, "Changing Living Arrangements: A Hazard Model of Transitions Among Household Types," The Rand Paper Series P-7060, The Rand Corporation, February 1985, p. 49.
3. The 1985 figures are unpublished results from the 1985 Current Population Survey, U.S. Bureau of the Census; the 1970 figures are from Kain, p. 19.
4. Kain, p. 16.
5. Kain, p. 18.
6. Fawn Vrazo, "Baby-Boomers Face A Future of Divorce," *The Philadelphia Inquirer*, 20 July 1986, page I-1.
7. Neil Bennett quoted in Fawn Vrazo, "Baby-Boomers Face a Future of Divorce," *The Philadelphia Inquirer*, 20 July 1986, page I-1.
8. Koray Tanfer and Marjorie C. Horn, "Nonmarital Cohabitation Among Young Women: Findings from a National Survey," paper presented at the annual meeting of the Population Association of America, 27–29 March 1984.
9. Paul C. Glick, "How American Families are Changing," *American Demographics*, January 1984, p. 23.

10. *Virginia Slims*, p. 35.

11. Duane F. Alwin, "Some Consequences of Recent Changes in Household Composition," *Economic Outlook USA*, Survey Research Center, University of Michigan, Volume 12, No. 2, Second Quarter 1985, pp. 42, 43.

12. National Center for Health Statistics, "Advance Report of Final Natality Statistics, 1984," *NCHS Monthly Vital Statistics Report*, Volume 35, No. 4, 18 July 1986.

13. National Center for Health Statistics, "Advance Report of Final Natality Statistics, 1980," *NCHS Monthly Vital Statistics Report*, Volume 31, No. 8, 30 November 1982.

14. U.S. Bureau of the Census, "Households, Families, Marital Status, and Living Arrangements: March 1986 (Advance Report)," *Current Population Reports*, series P-20, No. 412, November 1986, Table 5.

15. Virginia Slims, p. 35.

16. Ibid., pp. 35, 38.

17. U.S. Bureau of the Census, "Marital Status and Living Arrangements: March 1984," *Current Population Reports*, Series P-20, No. 399, July 1985, Table 1.

18. American Council of Life Insurance, "Households and Families," *DataTrack 4*, Summer 1978, p. 11.

19. National Center for Health Statistics, "Advance Report of Final Marriage Statistics, 1982," *NCHS Monthly Vital Statistics Report*, Volume 34, No. 3, 28 June 1985, Table 1.

20. U.S. Bureau of the Census, "Marital Status," p. 1.

21. National Center for Health Statistics, "Advance Report of Final Divorce Statistics, 1983," *NCHS Monthly Vital Statistics Report*, Volume 34, No. 9, 26 December 1985, Table 1.

22. National Center for Health Statistics, "Births, Marriages, Divorces, and Deaths for 1985," *NCHS Monthly Vital Statistics Report*, Volume 34, No. 12, 24 March 1986, p. 1.

23. National Center for Health Statistics, "Advance Report of Final Divorce Statistics, 1983," Tables 7, 10.

24. Arthur J. Norton and Jeanne E. Moorman, "Marriage and Divorce Patterns of U.S. Women in the 1980s," paper presented at the annual meeting of the Population Association of America, 4 April 1986.

25. National Center for Health Statistics, "Advance Report of Final Marriage Statistics, 1982," Tables 6, 7.

26. Andrew J. Cherlin, *Marriage Divorce Remarriage* (Cambridge, Massachusetts: Harvard University Press, 1981), p. 75.

27. Bryant Robey, "Demographic Trends Shaping Consumer Markets," speech given at the American Demographics Consumer Demographics Conference, Los Angeles, California, 22 September 1983.

28. James A. Weed, "Divorce: Americans' Style," *American Demographics*, March 1982, p. 14.

29. Paul C. Glick and Arthur J. Norton, "Marrying, Divorcing, and Living Together in the U.S. Today," *Population Bulletin*, Volume 32, No. 5 (Washington, D.C.: Population Reference Bureau, Inc., 1979), p. 21.

30. Glick, "How American Families are Changing," p. 22.

31. Ibid., p. 25.

32. John Milward, "Who Leader Writes a New Chapter," *USA Today*, 19 November 1985, p. D-1.

33. David E. Bloom, "The Labor Market Consequences of Delayed Childbearing," paper presented at the annual meetings of the American Statistical Association, Chicago, Illinois, 18 August 1986.

34. *Virginia Slims*, p. 60.

35. Wendy H. Baldwin and Christine Winquist Nord, "Delayed Childbearing in the U.S.: Facts and Fictions," *Population Bulletin*, Volume 39, No. 4 (Washington, D.C.: Population Reference Bureau, Inc., 1984), pp. 8, 9.

36. David E. Bloom, "Putting Off Children," *American Demographics*, September 1984, p. 30.

37. Levy and Michel, pp. 40, 41.

38. U.S. Bureau of the Census, "Fertility of American Women: June 1985," *Current Population Reports*, Series P-20, No. 406, June 1986, Table 2.

39. Anne R. Pebley and David E. Bloom, "Childless Americans," *American Demographics*, January 1982, p. 19.

40. Ibid.

41. Ibid., p. 20.

42. Pratt *et al.*, p. 28.

43. U.S. Bureau of the Census, "Fertility of American Women," Table 8.

44. National Committee for Adoption, *Adoption Factbook* (Washington, D.C.: National Committee for Adoption, 1985), pp. 13, 14.

45. National Center for Health Statistics, "Fecundity and Infertility in the United States, 1965–82," *NCHS Advance Data*, No. 104, 11 February 1985, p. 4.

46. Pratt *et al.*, p. 31.

47. Stephanie J. Ventura, Selma Taffel, and William D. Mosher, "Estimates of Pregnancies and Pregnancy Rates of the United States, 1976–81," *Public Health Reports*, Volume 100, No. 1, January/February 1985, p. 33.

48. Pratt *et al.*, p. 18.

49. Ventura *et al.*, p. 33.

50. Thomas S. Weisner and Bernice T. Eiduson, "The Children of the '60s as Parents," *Psychology Today*, January 1986, p. 65.

51. Ibid., p. 66.

52. Arthur J. Norton cited in "Children in Flux," Opener, *American Demographics*, September 1983, p. 14.

53. U.S. Bureau of the Census, "Household and Family Characteristics," p. 2.

54. George Masnick and Mary Jo Bane, *The Nation's Families: 1960–1990* (Boston, Massachusetts: The Joint Center for Urban Studies of MIT and Harvard University, Auburn House Publishing Company, 1980), p. 17.

55. Greg J. Duncan and Saul D. Hoffman, "A Reconsideration of the Economic Consequences of Marital Dissolution," *Demography*, Volume 22, No. 4, November 1985, pp. 485–497.

56. Arland Thornton and Deborah Freedman, "The Changing American Family," *Population Bulletin*, Volume 38, No. 4 (Washington, D.C.: Population Reference Bureau, Inc., 1983), p. 10.

57. Lynn K. White and Alan Booth, "The Quality and Stability of Remarriages: The Role of Stepchildren," *American Sociological Review*, Volume 50, No. 5, October 1985, pp. 689–698.

58. Suzanne M. Bianchi and Judith A. Seltzer, "Forgotten Children: Children Without Parents," paper presented at the annual meeting of the Population Association of America, 3–5 April 1986.

59. Cherlin, p. 85.

60. Bianchi and Seltzer.

61. U.S. Bureau of the Census, *Historical Statistics*, pp. 15, 49.

62. National Center for Health Statistics, "Births, Marriages, Divorces, and Deaths for 1985," p. 1.

63. Levi Strauss & Co., "Opinions About Motherhood: A Gallup/Levi's Maternity Wear National Poll of Pregnant Women and New Mothers," *Levi Strauss & Co. News*, 7 September 1983.

64. Pratt *et al.*, p. 29.

65. Joseph Lee Rodgers and J. Richard Udry, "The Seasonality of Birth and the Seasonality of Birth Planning," paper presented at the annual meeting of the Population Association of Amercia, March 1985.

66. National Center for Health Statistics, "Advance Report of Final Natality Statistics, 1984," Tables 9, 11.

67. U.S. Bureau of the Census, "Fertility of American Women," Table 1.

68. National Center for Health Statistics, "Advance Report of Final Natality Statistics, 1984," Table 2.

69. Judith Langer, "The New Mature Mothers," *American Demographics*, July 1985, p. 29.

70. Personal telephone conversation with Joseph H. Pleck, June 1985.

71. National Center for Health Statistics, "Advance Report of Final Natality Statistics, 1984," Table 3.

72. Lawrence Olson, *Costs of Children* (Lexington, Massachusetts: D. C. Heath and Company, 1983), p. 99.

73. Roger Lowenstein, "Expecting a Baby Soon? Expect to Spend a Pile of Money During the First Year..." *The Wall Street Journal*, 16 April 1986, Section 2, p. 1.

74. Leo J. Shapiro & Associates cited in Brad Edmondson, "How Big is the Baby Market?" *American Demographics*, December 1985, p. 27.

75. *Virginia Slims*, p. 60.

76. Norval D. Glenn and Sue Keir Hoppe, "Only Children as Adults," *Journal of Family Issues*, Volume 5, No. 3, September 1984, p. 378.

77. U.S. Bureau of the Census, "School Enrollment—Social and Economic Characteristics of Students: October 1985 (Advance Report)," *Current Population Reports*, Series P-20, No. 409, September 1986, Tables 1, 2.

78. U.S. Bureau of the Census, "Private School Enrollment, Tuition, and Enrollment Trends: October 1979," *Current Population Reports*, Special Studies, Series P-23, No. 121, September 1982, p. 3, Table 4.

79. Market Facts, Inc., *Saving for Children's Education* (Chicago, Illinois: Market Facts, Inc., 1985).

80. Anne McGrath, "New Ways to Fund a College Education," *U.S. News & World Report*, 3 February 1986, pp. 56, 57.

81. Mary Eckroth Mullins, "College Costs Outpacing Inflation," USA Snapshots, *USA Today*, 4 August 1986, p. E-1.

82. Friedan, p. 296.

83. What 1986 Buyers Want in Housing," *Professional Builder Magazine*, cited in the newsletter *Research Alert*, Volume 3, No. 20, 21 February 1986, p. 3.

84. Unpublished table from John R. Pitkin and George Masnick, Analysis and Forecasting, Inc., Cambridge, Massachusetts.

85. Wlliam C. Apgar, Jr., "Trends in Housing Demand and Preferences," *Real Estate Today*, September 1985, pp. 41–45.

86. U.S. League of Savings Institutions, pp. 16–21.

87. George Sternlieb and James W. Hughes, "The Good News About Housing," *American Demographics*, August 1985, p. 21.

88. *Virginia Slims*, p. 35.

89. Bureau of Labor Statistics, unpublished data for 1970 and 1984.

90. Maureen Dowd, "Many Women in Poll Value Jobs as Much as Family Life," *The New York Times*, 4 December 1983, pp. A1, A66.

91. The Roper Organization, Inc., *Roper Reports 85-2*, p. 239.

92. Ibid., p. 238.

93. Good Housekeeping Institute, *Women's Attitudes Toward*

Household Cleaning, A Good Housekeeping Institute Report, July 1983, p. 6.

94. *Virginia Slims,* p. 93.

95. F. Thomas Juster, "A Note on Recent Changes in Time Use," in F. Thomas Juster and Frank P. Stafford, eds., *Time, Goods and Well-Being* (Ann Arbor, Michigan: Survey Research Center, Institute for Social Research, University of Michigan, 1985), pp. 313–332.

96. William Michelson, *From Sun to Sun—Daily Obligations and Community Structure in the Lives of Employed Women and Their Families* (Totowa, New Jersey: Rowman & Allanheld, 1985), pp. 43–88.

97. U.S. Bureau of the Census, "Money Income," Table 16.

98. *Virginia Slims,* p. 93.

99. Good Housekeeping Institute, p. 9.

100. Peter Francese, "January White Sales," in People Patterns, syndicated column of the Cowles Syndicate, Inc., Des Moines, Iowa (now owned by King Features, New York), released 11–12 January 1986.

101. F. Thomas Juster, "Preferences For Work and Leisure," p. 16.

102. Personal telephone conversation with Judith Langer, June 1985.

103. Good Housekeeping Institute, *Cleaning Products Study,* A Good Housekeeping Institute Report, June 1983, p. 51.

104. Good Housekeeping Institute, *Women's Attitudes,* p. 7.

5. THE NEW CONSUMERS

1. *Money* magazine, *The Money Boomers: A Supplementary Report From Americans and Their Money 1984,* prepared for

Money (New York: Lieberman Research, Inc., March 1985), pp. 20, 27, 28, 30, 34.

2. Bureau of Labor Statistics, "Consumer Expenditure Survey Results from 1984," *Bureau of Labor Statistics News,* USDL 86-258, 22 June 1986, Table 3.

3. Geoffrey Colvin, "What the Baby-Boomers Will Buy Next," *Fortune,* 15 October 1984, pp. 28–34.

4. Bureau of Labor Statistics, "Consumer Expenditure Survey," Table 3.

5. Ibid.

6. Ibid.

7. William Dunn, "The Meat and Potatoes of Eating Out," *American Demographics,* January 1985, p. 35.

8. The Gallup Organization, *The 1983 Gallup Annual Report on Eating Out* (Princeton, New Jersey: The Gallup Organization, Inc., 1985), p. 58.

9. Rick Telberg, "What Happens When Consumers Like Eating at Home?" *Nation's Restaurant News,* 17 February 1986, p. 106.

10. Bureau of Labor Statistics, "Consumer Expenditure Survey," Table 3.

11. Ellen Farley, "The Movie Studios Hope Less Will Be More," *Business Week,* 13 January 1986, p. 13.

12. Kevin Anderson, "VCRs Will Rival TV in 10 years," *USA Today,* 27 January 1986, p. D-1.

13. Newspaper Advertising Bureau, Inc., *Movie Going in the United States* (New York: Newspaper Advertising Bureau, Inc., 1986), p. 2.

14. Adam Stagliano quoted in Maria Fisher, "The New Leisure Generation," *Adweek,* 15 August 1985, p. 3.

15. Grey Advertising, *Network 86* (New York: Grey Advertising, Inc., 1986), p. 5.

16. Joe Mandese, "Network TV Erosion Worsening; Prime-time CPMs Could Rise by 80%," *Adweek*, 24 February 1986, p. 1.

17. William Meyers, "Why Americans are Turning Off to TV Ads," *Adweek*, 4th Annual Badvertising Report, January 1986, p. B.R. 4.

18. Brad Edmondson, "Ryan Homes Have Brains," Business Reports, *American Demographics*, August 1985, p. 16.

19. Louis Harris & Associates, Inc., *Americans and the Arts*, Study No. 831011, A 1984 Survey of Public Opinion Conducted for Philip Morris, Inc. (New York: Louis Harris & Associates, Inc., 1984), Tables 1, 2.

20. Maria Fisher, "The New Leisure Generation," *Adweek*, 15 August 1985, p. 2.

21. United Media Enterprises, Inc., *Where Does the Time Go? The United Media Enterprises Report on Leisure in America* (New York: United Media Enterprises, Inc., 1982), pp. 19, 22.

22. The Gallup Organization, Inc., *The Gallup 1985 Annual Report on Book Buying* (Princeton, New Jersey: The Gallup Organization, Inc., 1985), p. 23.

23. William Dunn, "Selling Books," *American Demographics*, October 1985, pp. 40, 43.

24. The Gallup Organization, Inc., *The Gallup 1985 Annual Report on Book Buying*, p. 276.

25. Mediamark Research, Inc., "Magazine Audience Estimates: Spring 1986" (New York: Mediamark Research, Inc., 1986).

26. Louis Harris & Associates, Inc., *Americans and the Arts*, p. 57.

27. Virginia Ann Hodgkinson and Murray S. Weitzman, *The Charitable Behavior of Americans—A National Survey*, conducted by Yankelovich, Skelly, and White, Inc. (Washington, D.C.: Independent Sector, 1986), p. 1.

28. Bureau of Labor Statistics, "Consumer Expenditure Survey," Table 3.

29. Louis Harris & Associates, Inc., *Americans and the Arts*, p. 94.

30. American Association of Fund Raising Counsel, Inc., *Giving USA—Estimates of Philanthropic Giving in 1985 and the Trends They Show* (New York: AAFRC Trust for Philanthropy, 1986), p. 7.

31. The Gallup Organization, Inc., *Americans Volunteer 1985*, A Study Conducted for Independent Sector (Princeton, New Jersey: The Gallup Organization, Inc., 1986), pp. 10–12, 34.

32. Shearson Lehman Economics projections from "Where The Money Will Go," *Newsweek*, 24 March 1986, p. 5.

33. U.S. Travel Data Center, *National Travel Survey, 1984 Full Year Report* (Washington, D.C.: U.S. Travel Data Center, 1985), p. 9.

34. Jean Epping quoted in Fisher, p. 2.

35. Constanza Montana, "Career Couples Find Vacations Hard to Plan," *The Wall Street Journal*, 4 August 1986, Section 2, p. 1.

36. Market Opinion Research, *Participation in Outdoor Recreation Among American Adults and the Motivations Which Drive Participation*, for presentation to the President's Commission on Americans Outdoors (Detroit: Market Opinion Research, 1986), pp. 115–118.

37. Marriott Corporation, "Marriott Class At a First-Rate Price—National Survey Leads to Precedent-Setting Luxury Discount," press release of results from survey conducted by R. H. Bruskin & Associates, 5 February 1986.

38. Barbara I. Brown, "How The Baby Boom Lives," *American Demographics*, May 1984, p. 35.

39. John P. Robinson, "American Outdoor Recreation Trends: 1960–1983 (A Methodological Analysis of Data

from the 1982–83 National Recreation Survey)," University of Maryland Survey Research Center, March 1986.

40. Merle J. Van Horne, Laura B. Szwak, and Sharon A. Randall, "Outdoor Recreation Activity Trends—Insights From the 1982–83 Nationwide Recreation Survey," *Proceedings of Outdoor Recreation Trends Symposium II*, Myrtle Beach, South Carolina, 25–27 February 1985, Table 2.

41. The Roper Organization, *Roper Reports 85-2*, p. 324.

42. Van Horne *et al.*, "Outdoor Recreation Activity Trends."

43. Ibid.

44. Marc L. Yergin, "Who Goes to the Game?," *American Demographics*, July 1986, pp. 42–43.

45. U.S. Bureau of the Census, "Household Wealth and Asset Ownership: 1984," Data from the Survey of Income and Program Participation, Household Economic Studies, *Current Population Reports*, Series P-70, No. 7, July 1986, Table 5.

46. Robert B. Avery, Gregory E. Elliehausen, Glenn B. Canner, and Thomas A. Gustafson, "Survey of Consumer Finances, 1983: A Second Report," *Federal Reserve Bulletin*, December 1984, p. 859.

47. Federal Reserve Board, *Federal Reserve Bulletin*, Volume 72, No. 6, June 1986, Table A-40.

48. *Money* magazine, *Americans and Their Money 3, The Third National Survey from Money Magazine/1985* (New York: Time, Inc., 1985), pp. 136, 139, 144.

49. U.S. Bureau of the Census, "Household Wealth," Table 5.

50. *Money* magazine, *Americans and Their Money*, p. 106.

51. Dean Rotbart, "Stocks Have Climbed, But Usual Eupho-

ria Seems Oddly Absent," *The Wall Street Journal*, 27 November 1985, pp. 1, 16.

52. John J. Phelan, Jr., "1985 National Shareownership Study," an address before the Securities Industry Association, Boca Raton, Florida, 4 December 1985.

53. *Money* magazine, *The Money Boomers*, p. 25.

54. Market Facts, Inc., *Investment Risk* (Chicago: Market Facts, Inc., 1984), p. 2.

55. Fabian Linden, Gordon W. Green, Jr., and John F. Coder, *A Marketer's Guide to Discretionary Income*, A Joint Study by the Consumer Research Center, The Conference Board, and the U.S. Bureau of the Census, 1985, pp. 12–13, 22–23, 30–31, 34–35.

56. The American Society for Quality Control, *Consumer Perceptions Concerning the Quality of American Products and Services*, GO-85172, a study conducted by The Gallup Organization, Princeton, New Jersey, September 1985, pp. 17–18.

57. Mediamark Research, Inc., *Tobacco, Candy, Shopping*, Spring 1985, P-11, p. 209.

58. *Money* magazine, *The Money Boomers*, p. 43.

59. Randall Smith, "Sharp Rise in Video Shopping Shares Leaves Analysts Divided Over Companies' Prospects," Heard on the Street, *The Wall Street Journal*, 20 June 1986, p. 43.

60. "U.S. Drinks Less, Entertains More," Roper's America, *Adweek*, 24 February 1986, p. 17.

61. James Ogilvy, *The Experience Industry* (Menlo Park, California: SRI International, Values and Lifestyles Program, 1985), pp. ES-1, ES-2.

62. Doris Walsh, "Pier 1 Keeps Up," Business Reports, *American Demographics*, May 1986, pp. 16–17.

6. THE NEW BELIEVERS

1. U.S. Bureau of the Census, "Voting and Registration in the Election of November 1984 (Advance Report)," *Current Population Reports*, Series P-20, No. 397, January 1985, Table 1.

2. Jane Newitt, "The Decade of the Young Voter," *American Demographics*, September 1984, p. 19.

3. U.S. Bureau of the Census, "Voting," Tables a, b.

4. Lee Atwater quoted in David Boaz, ed., *Left, Right & Baby Boom* (Washington, D.C.: Cato Institute, 1986), p. 35.

5. Pat Caddell quoted in David Boaz, ed., *Left, Right & Baby Boom* (Washington, D.C.: Cato Institute, 1986), pp. 48–49.

6. Thomas Exter and Frederick Barber, "The Age of Conservatism," *American Demographics*, November 1986, pp. 30–37.

7. Newitt, p. 24.

8. The Gallup Organization, *Religion in America, 50 Years: 1935–1985*, The Gallup Report, Report No. 236, May 1985, p. 6.

9. Ibid., pp. 16, 22, 30, 40, 42, 50.

10. Tom W. Smith, "America's Religious Mosaic," *American Demographics*, June 1984, pp. 18–23.

11. Paul D. Kleppner quoted in David Boaz, ed., *Left, Right & Baby Boom* (Washington, D.C.: Cato Institute, 1986), p. 116.

7. THE NEW OLD

1. Eliot Glazer, "Feelings About Age, Part III" (New York: Cadwell Davis Partners, 1985).

2. Jacob S. Siegel and Cynthia M. Taeuber, "Demographic Perspectives on the Long-Lived Society," in "The Aging Society," *Daedalus*, issued as Volume 115, No. 1 of the Proceedings of the American Academy of Arts and Sciences, Winter 1986, p. 96.

3. "Median Retiree Age Drops, Study Shows," *St. Louis Post-Dispatch*, 24 July 1985, p. 11A (five-star edition).

4. Philip L. Rones, "Using the CPS to Track Retirement Trends Among Older Men," Research Summaries, *Monthly Labor Review*, February 1985, p. 47.

5. U.S. Bureau of the Census, "Projections of the Population," Table 6.

6. Leslie Ensor Stockman and June Fletcher, "A Maturing Market," *Builder*, June 1985, p. 73.

7. William Lazer, "Inside the Mature Market," *American Demographics*, March 1985, p. 22.

8. Jordan, Case & McGrath, Inc., *The 55+ Market: The Marketing Opportunity of the 1980's* (New York: Jordan, Case & McGrath, 1980), p. 4.

9. U.S. Bureau of the Census, "Demographic and Socioeconomic Aspects of Aging in the United States," *Current Population Reports*, Series P-23, No. 138, August 1984, p. 99; 1950 figure from personal telephone conversation with Census Bureau education specialist.

10. Lazer, p. 49.

11. U.S. Bureau of the Census, 1986 and 1981 Current Population Surveys, unpublished data.

12. U.S. Bureau of the Census, "After-Tax Money Income Estimates of Households: 1984," *Current Population Reports*, Special Studies, Series P-23, No. 147, July 1986, Table 1.

13. U.S. Bureau of the Census, "Household Wealth," Table 5.

14. Philip Longman, "Age Wars," *The Futurist*, January–February 1986, pp. 8–11.

15. United States General Accounting Office, *Social Security—Past Projections and Future Financing Concerns*, Report to Congressional Requesters, GAO/HRD-86-22, pp. 56–62.

16. Mary Kuntz, "It Wasn't Meant to be Fair," *Forbes*, 7 April 1986, p. 120.

17. Bureau of Labor Statistics, "Consumer Expenditure Survey," Table 3.

18. Marilyn M. McMillen, "Sex-Specific Equivalent Retirement Ages: 1940–2050," *Social Security Bulletin*, March 1984, p. 7.

19. Jeffrey D. Alderman, ABC News/Washington Post Poll, Survey Nos. 203, 206, 209, 10–13 November 1985.

20. Edwin A. Finn, Jr., "Instead of Planning for Retirement, Young Professionals Fret About It," *The Wall Street Journal*, 9 December 1985, Section 2, p. 1.

21. Deborah Chollet, "Financing Retirement Today and Tomorrow: The Prospect for America's Workers," paper presented at the Employee Benefit Research Institute Policy Forum, "America in Transition: Employee Benefits for the Future," Washington, D.C., 15 October 1986, Table 9.

22. Ibid., Table 8.

23. Employee Benefit Research Institute, "Women, Families and Pensions," *EBRI Issue Brief*, No. 49, December 1985, p. 8.

24. Donald G. Schmitt, "Today's Pension Plans: How Much Do They Pay?" *Monthly Labor Review*, December 1985, p. 19.

25. Chollet, Table 9.

26. Chollet, Table 8.

27. Chollet, Tables 7–9.

28. Arland Thornton and Deborah Freedman, "The Changing American Family: Living Arrangements and Relation-

ships with Kin," *Economic Outlook USA*, Volume 12, No. 2, Survey Research Center, Institute for Social Research, The University of Michigan, 2nd Quarter 1985, p. 36.

29. U.S. Bureau of the Census, "Marital Status and Living Arrangements," Table 2.

30. Martha Farnsworth Riche, "Retirement's Lifestyle Pioneers," *American Demographics*, January 1986, p. 42.

31. "How They Rank—1980 Census Results Ranked for States, Metropolitan Areas, and Cities of 50,000 or More," *American Demographics*, December 1983, p. 37.

32. Riche, p. 44.

33. Ibid., p. 54.

34. "Americans on Vacation," Status, *American Demographics*, November 1985, p. 16.

35. Bill Johnson, "Deluxe Travel Tours Offer Vacationers a Taste of the Exotic—and a Soft Bed," *The Wall Street Journal*, 22 July 1985, Section 2, p. 1.

36. Joseph F. Coates, "The Next 30 Years in Travel," *Proceedings of the U.S. Travel Data Center's Eleventh Annual Travel Outlook Forum*, New Orleans, 20 September 1985.

37. Ibid.

38. Arthur Levine and Jack Lindquist, "The Muppie-izing of America," *The New York Times*, 28 July 1985, p. E21.

8. WHAT THE BABY BOOM WILL DIE OF

1. National Center for Health Statistics, *Vital Statistics of the United States, 1982, Life Tables*, Volume II, Section 6, DHHS Pub. No. (PHS)85-1104 (Washington, D.C.: U.S. Government Printing Office, 1985), Tables 6-3, 6-a.

2. John M. Owen and James W. Vaupel, "An Exercise in

Life Expectancy," *American Demographics*, November 1985, pp. 37–38.

3. Lois M. Verbrugge, "From Sneezes to Adieux," *American Demographics*, May 1986, pp. 34–39, 53.

4. Ibid., p. 35.

5. Ibid.

6. Ibid., p. 36.

7. Ibid., p. 53.

8. National Center for Health Statistics, *Current Estimates from the National Health Interview Survey: United States, 1982*, Series 10, No. 150, DHHS Pub. No. (PHS)85-1578, September 1985, Table 26.

9. Ibid., Table 1.

10. Ibid., Table 57.

11. Glenn Collins, "Many in Work Force Care for Elderly Kin," *The New York Times*, 6 January 1986, p. B5.

12. Marilyn Doss Ruffin, "Contribution of the Family to the Economic Support of the Elderly," *Family Economics Review*, No. 4, U.S. Department of Agriculture, October 1984, p. 8.

13. Alice T. Day, "Who Cares? Demographic Trends Challenge Family Care for the Elderly," *Population Trends and Public Policy* (Washington, D.C.: Population Reference Bureau, September 1985), p. 4.

14. Ibid.

15. National Center for Health Statistics, "Aging in the Eighties, Age 65 Years and Over and Living Alone, Contacts with Family, Friends, and Neighbors, Preliminary Data From the Supplement on Aging to the National Health Interview Survey: United States, January–June 1984," *NCHS Advance Data*, Number 116, 9 May 1986, p. 3.

16. Ibid.

17. U.S. Bureau of the Census, "Demographic and Socioeconomic Aspects of Aging in the United States," p. 90.

18. Ibid., Table 7-9.

19. Ibid., p. 91.

20. Ibid.

21. "Harper's Index," *Harper's*, May 1986, p. 11.

22. Day, pp. 4-5.

23. Martha Farnsworth Riche, "The Nursing Home Dilemma," *American Demographics*, October 1985, p. 36.

24. Siegel and Taeuber, p. 106.

25. Employee Benefit Research Institute, "Financing Long-Term Care," *EBRI Issue Brief*, No. 48, November 1985, p. 1.

26. Ibid.

27. Ibid., p. 9.

28. Paul Wiligang quoted in Martha Farnsworth Riche, "The Nursing Home Dilemma," *American Demographics*, October 1985, p. 37.

29. Katie Sloan quoted in Martha Farnsworth Riche, "Retirement's Lifestyle Pioneers," *American Demographics*, January 1986, p. 50.

30. Joyce Jensen, "Health Care Alternatives," *American Demographics*, March 1986, p. 38.

31. National Center for Health Statistics, *Life Tables*, Table 6-2.

32. U.S. Bureau of the Census, "Projections of the Population," Table 6.

33. National Center for Health Statistics, *Life Tables*, Table 6-3.

34. Noreen Goldman and Graham Lord, "Sex Differences in Life Cycle Measures of Widowhood," *Demography*, Volume 20, No. 2, May 1983, p. 185.

35. Siegel and Taeuber, p. 103.

36. Lois M. Verbrugge, "Gender and Health: An Update on Hypotheses and Evidence," *Journal of Health and Social Behavior*, Volume 26, No. 3, September 1985, p. 177.

37. Siegel and Taeuber, pp. 97, 98.

38. U.S. Bureau of the Census, "Projections of the Population," Table 6.

INDEX

3 1542 00088 8754

338.5443
R961o

DATE DU

338.5443
R961o

Russell
100
predictions for
the baby boom

WITHDRAWN

Haas Library
Muhlenberg College
Allentown, Pennsylvania